TEACHING DEVELOPMENTAL GYMNASTICS

Teaching Developmental Gymnastics

Skills to Take through Life

Garland O'Quinn, Jr.

Photographs by E. Jessica Hickman

 University of Texas Press, Austin

First Edition, 1990

Requests for permission to reproduce material from this work should
be sent to Permissions, University of Texas Press, Box 7819, Austin,
Texas 78713–7819.

∞The paper used in this publication meets the minimum requirements
of American National Standard for Information Sciences—Permanence
of Paper for Printed Library Materials, ANSI Z39.48–1984.

Library of Congress Cataloging-in-Publication Data

O'Quinn, Garland.
    Teaching developmental gymnastics : skills to take through life / by
Garland O'Quinn, Jr. ; photographs by E. Jessica Hickman. — 1st ed.
        p.   cm.
    Bibliography: p.
    Includes index.
    ISBN 0–292–78101–6 (alk. paper). — ISBN 0–292–78104–0 (pbk. :
alk. paper)
    1. Gymnastics—Study and teaching.   I. Title.
GV461.069   1990
796.41′07—dc20   89–31936
                                                                CIP

Drawings by Sally Blakemore

*To my daughter, Lanita, whose laughter and love make the
world a better place,*

*and to my son, Danny, whose skills and good humor have
kept this program alive and well,*

*and to Sam and Carie and all the world's children,
I dedicate this program.*

Contents

Acknowledgments

All of us learn from each other. I have had the good fortune of being influenced by many wonderful people. Just a few of them are mentioned below.

Thomas Maloney was my gymnastics coach at West Point. He had a great influence upon my life as well as the lives of the many other young men he coached during his thirty years at West Point.

During my competitive years it was my good fortune to have Jamile Ashmore as my teammate. Jamile was completely unselfish toward me and added greatly to my understanding of gymnastics and life.

During my years of graduate school at Pennsylvania State University, Bruce Young was a fellow student and friend who made great contributions to my understanding of how learning takes place in the nervous system.

Liselott Diem developed a wonderful program of sequential gymnastics, which acts as a model for physical education. Her program has been the model for Developmental Gymnastics.

Bill Wahlman directed the summer recreation program at Portales, New Mexico, where this program was born. He encouraged me to continue my work with young children.

The following members of the Education Committee of the United States Gymnastics Federation were extremely helpful and encouraging in bringing this revision to the public: Susan True, James Nance III, Eric Malmberg, Patty Hacker, and Alan Tilove. They have taken the spirit of this program and expanded the curriculum for the higher grades.

Although I never met them, I am grateful to Sinichi Suzuki and Maria Montessori, who have left a legacy of respect for the child and love for the next generation, which enhances this program and all that comes after.

A special thanks to all of the children who demonstrated for the photographer. Their names are Ana García, Orin and Loren Darrington, Jake Mase, Holly and Colin Stokes, Esther Sunukjian, and Azurea Vredenburg.

Thanks go to the staff at the University of Texas Press for their patience and assistance in bringing this book to publication.

Special thanks go to my wife, Ginny, who has been so patient and loving through the many years that I have worked on this program.

1. Introduction

Children truly enjoy physical play. Wiggling, running, and swinging their arms are expressions of freedom and sheer kinesthetic pleasure. Never again will they be so intensely interested and willing to take on challenges that involve physical play.

Feeling Alive

Children enjoy physical play as much as or more than they like candy. Their bodies thrive on the new and spontaneous feelings that come from hanging by their arms, swinging, climbing, balancing, and rolling. Movement gives children the feeling of being alive and provides the means by which they are able to participate in life.

The Joy of Success

Success in meeting a physical challenge provides that inner joy which makes us want to continue. No one likes to fail and nothing turns a child away from participating and learning as quickly as failure.

The joy of success is the most powerful motivator for learning. When children receive that "just right" physical challenge they will perform the activity over and over again in sheer delight. Children who are successful will search out new tasks and will approach challenges with a positive attitude, instead of acting defensive and avoiding participation. The child's attitude toward the world changes to one of interest and exploration. Giving a child the opportunity to succeed can truly change a life.

The Growing Edge

All of us have, so to speak, climbed the ladder of physical skill up to a certain point and there we sit. The very next step on the ladder represents our growing edge. It is an activity or a skill that is very close to our present ability but one that will put us in a better position to continue our journey up the ladder.

Step by Step on the Ladder of Skills

When a child is presented a task that is too far up the ladder, when too many steps are left out, the child has an insurmountable obstacle and learning is apt to stop or be diverted into some other area of activity. The ideal task for the most rapid learning is represented by the very next step on the ladder of skills.

The activities in this book have been arranged so that they represent the steps of a ladder. When they are taken in sequence, one step at a time, learning will progress at the most effective rate.

Skills to Take Children through Life

By and large, the balance, coordination, and ability that children learn by age 10 is what they will have to carry them through life. Few adults can climb a rope or balance on a log better now than they could at age 10. So, as parents and teachers, this is our opportunity to provide the next generation with the physical education they will need throughout their lives.

Children Need Adult Help

The "free play" environment on beautifully painted playgrounds helps the natural athlete far more than it does the rest of us. Most children will reach less than 50 percent of their potential. The reason for this is that the aggressive and highly skilled child will dominate the playground, providing a model that other children cannot match. Many children who might have great potential if properly nurtured will retreat to a more orderly place on the playground to prevent being run over or put down. The only way for children to reach their potential is to be nurtured and supervised by a trained adult.

You can provide this opportunity for your children by carefully following the instructions in this book, and you can get help through the American Association of Educational Gymnastics Teachers (further explanation in Chapter 6).

About Developmental Gymnastics

The Developmental Gymnastics program is arranged in sequential upward steps. This arrangement in the proper order for maturation and learning provides a happy and loving atmosphere for children.

Challenge without Threat

By being provided that "just right" challenge, the children are happy to take part and they enjoy the success that comes from participation. Children are not turned away by the threat of failure, but they are encouraged by the successful completion of the task.

Self-confidence

As the children feel the pattern of success, it becomes a great source of self-confidence. Children participate willingly because they feel that they belong in the program. Children feel more and more comfortable with physical challenge and develop the attitude "I can do it."

Self-awareness

Children come to know themselves through the kinesthetic feelings of movement within their body. What their eyes see and what their ears hear is matched up with what their body feels. This self-awareness is valuable as they strive to understand themselves and to communicate with others.

Safety

The Developmental Gymnastics program is safe because of the sequential order in which the activities are presented. It is very important to introduce activities beginning with step 1 and to allow children ample time to play again and again with that step until it becomes a fluent and subconscious activity. Only then should one go on to the next step in the sequence.

Teachers' Association

The many teachers trained in Developmental Gymnastics are so convinced of its continued importance for the education of children that they have formed the American Association of Educational Gymnastics Teachers. See Chapter 6 for details of how they can assist you.

How This Book Is Organized

NOVICE PROGRAM: *Introduction to the world of physical skill and body control*

Introduce children to the program at this level regardless of age. The novice level develops the most basic balance and posture positions and movements. Children may begin as early as age 3 but no age is too late.

INTERMEDIATE PROGRAM: *Expand and explore the abilities of the body*

Children must not enter this level before they have mastered the novice level, including the many variations. Once children know the basic postures and balance positions, they will want to expand their activities to include new challenges. Here children feel the excitement of exploration and adventure.

ADVANCED PROGRAM: *Refine and complete the adventure*

Children who have mastered the intermediate level will be eager to continue. The accomplishment of these advanced skills will give children a sense of completion and fulfillment. The self-confidence and accomplishment will allow most to go on to other adventures. A few will want to pursue gymnastics into the world of competitive sport.

Basic Body Positions

Because certain basic body positions reoccur in gymnastic activities, it is useful to give these postures a name:

Pike

Squat

Tuck

Balanced
Landing
Position

Straddle

Gymnastic
Salute

The Five Physical Apparatus

A physical development program for children should ensure stimulation of all the kinesthetic senses as well as the muscle systems. The five Developmental Gymnastics apparatus have been chosen because they represent the simplest set of activities that will ensure all the necessary muscle and sensory stimulation and growth. *Be not overwhelmed.* One should not turn away feeling overwhelmed by the need for a great deal of equipment. An individual mat is all one needs to start. Then a substitute can often be found for the other apparatus.

Individual Mats

The mat activities provide for development of a great many body postures and balance positions. The mats also offer opportunity for the development of flexibility and agility.

   Individual mats also provide for a spatial separation of the children to ensure plenty of freedom to perform and to fall without hitting other children. Individual mats adequately separated contribute a great deal to safety.

Springboard

An important kinesthetic sensation is free flight in space. The springboard provides this sensation of freedom in a safe manner. Children are never allowed to "flip" in the air, but rather simply soar in an upright position. Nevertheless, the body must prepare itself for landings and the sensory system learns to anticipate the muscle tone necessary to make a smooth and balanced landing.

Low Horizontal Bar

The low horizontal bar provides for development of muscles in the arms, shoulders, and abdomen. Normally, activities in our society offer little opportunity for development of these muscle groups.

The low horizontal bar also provides for development of the inner ear. The semicircular canals, which provide orientation in space, cannot receive full development without the rotation in various planes. This apparatus should not be left out of the child's experience.

Tumbling Table/Wedge

The tumbling table is very important as an aid to success. Many children will find it easy to turn head over heels or to vault over this apparatus when they might otherwise not have success at these activities. For many children this apparatus provides that all-important "first time" experience of many tumbling movements.

Beam

The beam provides the best opportunity for children to develop the subconscious control of balance. The narrow base of support requires the body's systems for posture adjustment to be constantly alert for response.

To Obtain Equipment

Write to Physical Fun Products, Box 4548, Austin, TX 78765, for a catalog of equipment used in this program. 1-800-955-1439.

For Parents

As a parent, you are naturally interested in giving your child a good start in life. In this regard nothing is more important for children to possess than self-confidence and self-esteem. You will want your child to participate in programs that provide the feelings of success. Developmental Gymnastics was designed specifically to help children feel good about themselves as they develop their physical skills.

The Joy of Learning

Few things make children happier than learning something new, feeling a new physical sensation, and finding out what their body can do. If we will nurture and encourage a child's natural abilities, his or her love for learning will continue throughout life.

Plenty of Time

The activities in Developmental Gymnastics are very interesting and exciting to children. When children are not rushed toward too high a level of difficulty, they delight in taking part and look forward to their next gymnastics lesson.

It is very important not to rush your children's development. Hugs rather than pushes are the encouragement that brings out the child's natural skills. Children will respond to insistence and threat, but the response is to the adult and the pressure rather than to the subject matter.

Observation Is a Form of Participation

Quite often a child will sit quietly and observe the actions of others during an entire play period. This is no cause for alarm. Observation is an important form of participation.

One might mistakenly believe that "nothing is being accomplished." This child, however, during some other part of the day, will usually copy the observed movements. It is much better to allow the children freedom to observe than to constantly insist that they physically participate.

One Step at a Time

Whether you teach your child or he or she attends classes elsewhere, you should insist that your child has plenty of opportunity to play with each step in the Developmental Gymnastics program and all of its many variations. Many repetitions are far more important than much lecture and explanation. The many repetitions provide a deep background of experience upon which more refined skills can easily be developed in later life.

Refinement Can Come Later

During the child's early years it is important that the program have a spontaneous play atmosphere. This allows the child to develop an inner motivation and an appreciation for physical activity. Refinement into competitive sport can come later. Putting too much emphasis on what an activity looks like to the teacher or to a judge can cause the child to "burn out" and lose interest before reaching maximum potential.

The Reward of Self-confidence

The self-confidence that comes from successful physical play has a powerful effect on the lives of children. "Watch me, Mommie," "Watch me, Daddy," is a common response of children who feel good about themselves. They feel successful and they want to share that feeling with their parents. Having control of their body provides a sense of fulfillment, a feeling that "I can do it." In later years this inner self-confidence can provide the basis for success in a profession, in business, and in life.

You Can Get Help in Choosing a Program

The American Association of Educational Gymnastics Teachers can help you find a teacher or evaluate programs in your area. Contact them at the address listed in Chapter 6.

For Day Care Personnel

Our society has changed so much in the last ten years that we have hardly had time to adjust. One of the changes that has great implications for the day care center is that the children you serve have very little time with older brothers and sisters or with any older children. These older children once served as the teachers of physical play for the younger children. That is true no longer, and the responsibility now falls to the adult caregiver.

Much of the motivation for physical play comes through the imagination of the child, a state of mind that adults have long since grown past. This makes it difficult for some adults to identify with children's play. A few, however, can see themselves in the children and will enjoy guiding children through physical play.

Imagery—the World of Children

Since the children have no personal experience to draw from, they fill their world with the images of stories read to them or TV stories that they have seen or heard. These images are tied into reality so far as the child is concerned. To say that the mat you are standing on is "hot" can cause a far greater and more complete response than saying "lift your feet quickly." Therefore, when you offer children experiences in movement, if you can put the challenge in the form of an image with which they identify, it will be far more effective than simply reading the explanation from the book. As you find an image that works extremely well with children, please write it out in the margin under the activity. And please let us know about it so that we can add your "suggested imagery" under the activities in future editions.

The Individual Mat

The most important physical apparatus in children's play is simply an individual mat that will provide physical separation from other children. Space to stretch out, jump, and swing the arms is very important to safety as well as good learning.

Safety Spots (An Alternative to Standing in Line)

A dislike for waiting in line is not just a child's problem; it is a human problem. No one enjoys waiting in line. It is not a child's "fault" for being fidgety and getting in trouble while waiting in line. Therefore, the alternative to waiting in line is to be occupied with constructive activity whenever possible. Safety spots provide at least some of that constructive activity. Children are asked to travel around a circular course of simple obstacles marked by "safety spots." Then one of the five apparatus can be placed somewhere in the circle to offer the special challenge of the day.

The Noncognitive Aspects of Learning

Modern research on the brain tells us that children cannot learn physical skill from verbal lecture. Explanations are primarily for setting up the conditions under which the physical play can occur. The most important ingredient for learning a physical skill is the physical play itself. Physical activity should, therefore, comprise most of the gymnastics lesson.

Safety

For many people the word *gymnastics* brings to mind flipping in the air. *Developmental Gymnastics does not involve this kind of risk activity.* The primary rule for safety is to follow the steps beginning with step 1. Do not move up the scale of difficulty until the child has mastered that step along with all of its variations. A complete list of safety rules is included in Chapter 6.

Teacher Certification

Should you desire a more complete understanding than can be obtained from just reading this book, a certification program has been specifically designed for those who wish to teach Developmental Gymnastics. See the last section in this Introduction for more details.

Teachers' Supplement

Chapter 6 comprises a supplement for teachers and offers a deeper discussion of how to deal with children in the physical play setting. Be sure to read through this section, especially the section on *safety*, before implementing your program.

For Schoolteachers

Gymnastics has become popular not as an educational activity but as an Olympic sport. Therefore, our concept has been of flips in the air and dangerous, risky tricks. Developmental Gymnastics is not flips and dangerous tricks; rather it is that part of gymnastics which can safely and effectively be taught to *all* of the children in our schools.

Safety

In order to ensure safety, all risky tricks have been taken out of this program. Yet, it is still important to teach the activities in the order they are listed. Begin with step 1 regardless of the age of the children.

Primary Grades

The children in kindergarten and first grade can spend all fall working on one or maybe two new steps. Concentrate on many repetitions and on covering all of the variations.

Elementary Grades

Children in the second grade and up will probably cover two or more steps in a season. Children who have not previously had Developmental Gymnastics should always be introduced to the program at step 1, but allow the children in higher grades to move faster up the scale to prevent them from becoming bored.

Then simulate the action without the apparatus. In this way all the children will receive a kinesthetic preview of what the movement will feel like. This procedure greatly increases the success rate when the children actually approach the apparatus.

Variations in Ability and Experience

You will always have a few children who require extra time to master the skills and a few who can already accomplish the skills before they are taught. These two groups of children provide a very real challenge for the teacher because, although they comprise only a small percentage of the total, they are often the most visible or the most verbal. Warming up with the easier skills will tend to bring the slower children into the group; and, through individual comments and instruction, the more highly skilled children can be allowed to attempt skills that match their own individual growing edge. Without question the teacher's greatest challenge is to deal with these two extremes in the same class.

Individual Mats and Fall Zones

Another important safety procedure is to provide each child with plenty of space—a zone within which he or she can jump, swing arms, and fall without hitting another child.

Physical Practice without Apparatus (Kinesthetic Preview)

Children cannot learn physical skill from lecture. Therefore, we must provide a physical experience for every child during our explanation of an apparatus skill. Have all the children spread out (on individual mats if possible) and put them in imaginary positions to simulate the apparatus being taught.

Teacher Certification

Those teachers who would like a more complete experience than can be obtained from just reading this book can take a certification course in Developmental Gymnastics. These courses are sponsored by the American Association of Educational Gymnastics Teachers. Further details can be found in the next section.

Teachers' Supplement

Before implementing a gymnastics program, be sure to read through the teachers' supplement in Chapter 6, especially the section on *safety*.

Certification in Developmental Gymnastics

The American Association of Educational Gymnastics Teachers (AAEGT) has been organized to ensure the quality of teacher certification, to record transcripts, and to guide the development of curriculum for teachers of Developmental Gymnastics. For information call 1-800-955-1439.

A Weekend Course

Each certification course in Developmental Gymnastics consists of sixteen hours of training, usually conducted over one weekend. The curriculum has been divided into three levels: novice, intermediate, and advanced. All teachers begin with the novice certification course.

Novice Certification

The novice program is intended to introduce gymnastic activities at the most basic level, including postures, locomotion, and very simple activities. Yet, this is the most important course because it provides the foundation upon which all later skill and instruction will be based.

During the novice certification course, teachers learn to feel confident in the physical activity environment. Teachers are not required to perform tricks, but rather learn to guide others in basic physical activity. This certification prepares the teacher to work with preschool children.

Intermediate Certification

The intermediate certification course prepares the teacher to work with the primary grades (kindergarten and first grade). Also included are techniques for working with classes of children in the public or private schools.

Advanced Certification

The advanced course prepares teachers to work with children in the elementary grades (second and higher). Teachers learn skills up to and including the cartwheel. Both teachers and children get a feeling of fulfillment in completing this course. They sense that at last they have arrived in the world of gymnastics.

Sponsors of the Certification Courses

The American Association of Educational Gymnastics Teachers will conduct the certification course in your community. The sponsors of certification courses are usually one or more of the following:
   City recreation departments
   Public school systems
   YMCAs, YWCAs
   Parochial school systems
   Community education programs
   University continuing education programs
   Day care businesses

2. Novice Program:
Students in Preschool and Grades K and 1

Novice Mat Activities

Upright Balance

Balancing involves reducing the base of support, thus challenging the body to maintain upright orientation and control.

This activity stimulates the body's reflex system and aids in the development of posture.

1. ☐ Introduced and understood
   ☐ Performs basic skill
   ☐ Conditioned response with variations

2. ☐ Introduced and understood
   ☐ Performs basic skill
   ☐ Conditioned response with variations

3. ☐ Introduced and understood
   ☐ Performs basic skill
   ☐ Conditioned response with variations

1. The Friendly Crab

DESCRIPTION:

Sit on individual mat. Raise one foot at a time, then one hand at a time to balance on seat. This is the *seat balance.* Then bring feet and hands down onto floor and raise hips so that seat does not touch floor. This is the *friendly crab.*

VARIATIONS:

While in the *seat balance* can you clap your feet together? Touch toes together? Heels together?

Can you cross your legs? Raise your arms? Pump your feet as if you were riding a bicycle?

While being a *friendly crab* can you raise one foot in the air and wave at another crab? Raise one hand and wave?

Can you hold one foot up and scratch it with one hand?

IMAGERY:

Crab in his hole in the sand hears his alarm clock, wakes up, stretches in a *seat balance,* turns around to look at his alarm clock, takes a walk on the beach, waves at friends, hears a big bird coming after him, runs back to his home in the sand.

2. Knee Balance

DESCRIPTION:

Sit on heels with toes pointing backward. Raise body to comfortable stance with arms outward for balance.

VARIATIONS:

Can you lean from side to side, raising first one leg then the other?

Can you do this with your hands on your hips?

Can you stretch one leg to the side and balance with the toe?

Can you put the opposite hand down and raise the toe off the floor?

Can you hold one leg up behind you and put your hands on the floor for balance?

Can you keep the leg behind you off the floor and raise one hand up?

Now, can you raise both hands up?

3. The Mechanical Toy

DESCRIPTION:

Stand comfortably with feet slightly apart and arms held out slightly from body. Walk slowly by leaning shoulders and body from side to side and momentarily balancing on one foot at a time.

VARIATIONS:

Can you walk forward a few steps?

Can you walk backward a few steps?

Can you hold your arms in front of you?

Can you hold your arms bent at the elbows?

Can you wave one arm mechanically?

Can you slowly step in turning movements until you turn all the way around?

IMAGERY:

The *mechanical toy* takes a walk, sees friends and waves, accidentally gets stuck while balanced on one leg. Arms start to move mechanically one way and then the other. Finally, it comes back to both feet and resumes its walk.

Falling and Landing

Learning to roll after falling is a very important safety technique. These various types of rolls will prepare children to better survive unexpected falls. These activities should be repeated a number of times so that the patterns become subconsciously controlled.

1. ☐ Introduced and understood
   ☐ Performs basic skill
   ☐ Conditioned response with variations

2. ☐ Introduced and understood
   ☐ Performs basic skill
   ☐ Conditioned response with variations

3. ☐ Introduced and understood
   ☐ Performs basic skill
   ☐ Conditioned response with variations

1. Back Rocker

DESCRIPTION:
From sitting on floor rock backward, lifting feet above the head.

CAUTION:
Tilt head toward chest so that head will not fall back against mat. (Children who have trouble keeping their head from tilting backward should be asked to hold a handkerchief between their chin and chest.)

VARIATIONS:
Can you climb with your feet like a squirrel on a spinning wheel?
Can you pretend to walk up the wall and across the ceiling?
Can you rock back three times in a row?
Can you look to one side as you begin and finish looking that direction?
Can you look behind you and finish turned around to face the opposite wall?

2. Seat Roll

DESCRIPTION:

Take *all-fours position* with hands and knees on mat. Allow right hip to come to mat while left hand leaves mat and follows body as it turns left to sitting position facing opposite direction from starting. Continue rolling over seat as right hand crosses over body and back to *all-fours position*.

VARIATIONS:

Can you roll back in the opposite direction?

Can you roll slowly and carefully?

Can you roll a little faster?

How fast can you go and still keep good control?

Can you start on your seat and roll across all fours back to your seat?

Can you start from standing on your knees with body erect?

3. Puppy Dog Roll

DESCRIPTION:

From *all-fours position* sit back so that seat touches heels and bring elbows and forearms to mat in front of body. Body is now in the *puppy dog position* with head down and back rounded. Lean toward the right, catching body with right hip, then right shoulder, and roll across back and return to *puppy dog position*.

VARIATIONS:

Can you roll slowly and carefully?

Can you roll a little faster?

Can you roll in the opposite direction?

Can you balance while on your back and wiggle your feet as though your friend were tickling your tummy?

Inverted Agility

Feeling confident that the arms can hold the weight of the body is one important purpose of these activities. They build arm and shoulder strength and also contribute to orientation in space because the visual picture is not upright.

The requirement for quick motions helps to develop dexterity and helps to make the body nimble and ready to respond.

1. ☐ Introduced and understood
   ☐ Performs basic skill
   ☐ Conditioned response with variations

2. ☐ Introduced and understood
   ☐ Performs basic skill
   ☐ Conditioned response with variations

3. ☐ Introduced and understood
   ☐ Performs basic skill
   ☐ Conditioned response with variations

1. Leg Lifter

DESCRIPTION:

Begin on hands and knees. Then raise hips up and knees off mat. From this *all-fours position* raise one leg up behind.

VARIATIONS:

While holding one leg up, can you hop around like a dog with a splinter in its foot?

How high can you kick the free leg?

Can you kick the free leg so high that the other foot comes off the mat?

Can you raise the opposite leg?

IMAGERY:

A little puppy goes out to play. It gets a splinter in its foot and has to carry the hurt foot in the air behind it. The puppy goes to the veterinarian, who takes the splinter out. Now the puppy can go back home well and happy.

2. Leg Switch

DESCRIPTION:

Begin in *all-fours position* as with *leg lifter*. Lift one leg up behind. Then kick free leg up high and quickly switch legs so that other leg is up and first leg is down.

VARIATIONS:

How high can you go?

How fast can you switch?

Can you kick the free leg outward to the side?

Can you switch legs twice before one comes down to catch you?

Can you kick both feet up behind at the same time like a mule?

IMAGERY:

A mule is eating grass in the pasture when suddenly a bee flies over and stings it on the rump. The sting scares the mule and it kicks both feet up behind it and goes "hee haw."

3. Straddle Switch

DESCRIPTION:

Begin on *all-fours* with legs in *straddle position*. Lift one foot outward and up off floor. Then allow that foot to come back to floor as opposite foot goes outward and up. By alternating one foot, then the other, create a switching action.

VARIATIONS:

Can you switch the feet four times? Eight times?

Can you make the *straddle* even wider?

Can you keep your legs straight?

Can you lift your legs higher?

Can you lift both feet at once?

Can you bring both feet from the *straddle* to clap the feet together before they return to the floor in a *straddle?*

Inverted Balance

To maintain balance and orientation while upside down is the purpose of these exercises. These activities help to integrate inner ear activity with visual images.

1. ☐ Introduced and understood
       ☐ Performs basic skill
       ☐ Conditioned response with variations

2. ☐ Introduced and understood
       ☐ Performs basic skill
       ☐ Conditioned response with variations

3. ☐ Introduced and understood
       ☐ Performs basic skill
       ☐ Conditioned response with variations

1. Head Touch

DESCRIPTION:

   Start on hands and knees. Rock backward so that seat touches heels and bring hands close to knees. Lean down so that head touches mat.

VARIATIONS:

   Can you raise one leg off the mat? The other leg?

   Can you raise one hand off the mat? Both hands off the mat?

   Can you push against the mat with your toes and straighten your legs? Now can you raise one hand? Both hands?

   Can you turn around so that when you look back between your legs you see your friends? Can you wave to them?

2. Knee Meets Elbow

DESCRIPTION:

Start on knees, sitting on heels with hands alongside knees. Do not move hands from this place on mat. Bend forward and place hairline of head on mat and raise hips so that legs are straight. Now raise one knee and place it on corresponding elbow.

HINTS:

The elbows often fall outward and are unstable. Stability is improved by pressing elbows inward. Children can practice placing elbow on knee while sitting upright on mat.

VARIATIONS:

Can you put the other knee on the other elbow?

While one knee is on the elbow can you tap the supporting foot?

Can your knees take turns climbing up on the elbows?

3. Tripod

DESCRIPTION:

Begin as in *knee meets elbow.* One knee is placed on elbow and held there while other knee is raised to other elbow.

VARIATIONS:

Can you stay balanced in a *tripod* until I count to 3?

Can you stay balanced until I count to 6? To 10?

Can you wiggle your feet?

Can you clap your feet together?

Upright Agility

The purpose of these activities is to develop the ability to land on balance from a variety of aerial positions. They also develop agility, dexterity, and the ability to take a variety of positions while in the air.

1. Knee Slapper

DESCRIPTION:
Jump upward into air and quickly bring knees upward; slap legs near knees with hands.

VARIATIONS:
Can you slap both knees at the same time?
Can you slap the knees twice before landing?
Can you slap your knees and then land facing to one side?
Can you do the *knee slapper* three times in a row?
What else can you do while doing the *knee slapper?*

1. ☐ Introduced and understood
☐ Performs basic skill
☐ Conditioned response with variations

2. ☐ Introduced and understood
☐ Performs basic skill
☐ Conditioned response with variations

3. ☐ Introduced and understood
☐ Performs basic skill
☐ Conditioned response with variations

2. Ankle Slapper

DESCRIPTION:

Leap upward; then quickly bring legs and feet up so that hands can touch ankles.

VARIATIONS:

Can you slap both ankles at the same time?

Can you keep your knees together and bring ankles outward?

Can you spread your knees apart and reach down between them to touch your ankles?

3. Twist and Leap

DESCRIPTION:

Stand with knees slightly bent and turn head and shoulders to face one side. Raise arms and leap upward allowing feet to come under shoulders and land *on balance.*

VARIATIONS:

Can you catch your balance and not have to take another step?

Can you leap higher?

Can you twist farther before you leap? Can you still catch your balance?

Who can twist in the opposite direction?

Who can twist so far that your feet land facing backward?

Who can twist even farther and still keep your balance when your feet land?

IMAGERY:

There was a little boy (girl) toy that wanted to turn around, so the toy twisted its shoulders and looked around, then it leaped up and landed facing to one side. It twisted and leaped again. It just kept twisting and leaping until it was facing the way it wanted to go.

Rolling Over Forward

Turning over the head requires a development of strength and maturity to ensure safety. Therefore, the novice movements are used to prepare the arms, shoulders, and trunk prior to actually turning over. The *novice inverted balance* sequence is also important to strengthen the neck prior to turning over forward.

1. ☐ Introduced and understood
   ☐ Performs basic skill
   ☐ Conditioned response with variations

2. ☐ Introduced and understood
   ☐ Performs basic skill
   ☐ Conditioned response with variations

3. ☐ Introduced and understood
   ☐ Performs basic skill
   ☐ Conditioned response with variations

1. Scamper

DESCRIPTION:

Start on hands and knees, then raise knees off mat to *all-fours position.* Now walk on hands and feet forward to end of mat.

VARIATIONS:

Can you scamper sideways? Backward?

Can you turn around and around?

Can you turn in the opposite direction so you will not get dizzy?

IMAGERY:

A little monkey was pacing back and forth in its cage. It would scamper to one end, then turn around and scamper to the other end. One day the zoo keeper left the door open, so the monkey went to the door and carefully looked out, but it was so big outdoors that it decided to just go around the outside of its cage and then jump right back in. And that is what it did. Now it is back in its cage safe and sound.

2. Back Rocker

DESCRIPTION:

Sit on mat with feet forward and knees bent, arms against legs, hands on mat. Rock backward pulling knees and feet over head. Then rock feet and legs forward and come back to sitting position.

VARIATIONS:

When you rock back can you straddle your legs and look at the ceiling?

Can you hold a cubie (bean bag) between your feet when you rock back?

Can you hold the cubie up in the air, then drop it over your head?

Can you pull your knees with your hands?

Can you pull only one knee and leave the other leg straight?

IMAGERY:

I was rocking in my rocking chair, as happy as can be. One day that silly rocking chair tipped on top of me. (Children rock during poem, then on last verse they raise legs up, then fall to one side.)

3. Look Behind

DESCRIPTION:

Start from *squat position* so that hands are on mat, buttocks are sitting on heels, and knees are between elbows. Then raise hips overhead and tuck chin and head under to look back between legs.

VARIATIONS:

Who can see the wall behind them?

Who can turn around so that they see a friend?

Can you see another friend?

Can you turn all the way around?

Can you see the ceiling?

Can you hop forward like a bunny before you look between your legs?

IMAGERY:

A bunny was hopping along looking for carrots. Suddenly, it heard something behind it; it carefully raised its tail and looked back between its legs to see what it was. It was Farmer McGregor, so quick as it could the bunny hopped back to its hole in the ground.

Rolling Over Backward

Rolling over backward is one of the more difficult maneuvers because it requires taking all of the weight over the head without injury to the neck. Therefore, both novice and intermediate activities are used just to prepare the body. The *novice inverted balance* sequence is also prerequisite for rolling over backward. One may notice that this is the third time the *back rocker* is used. This indicates how important this activity is to safety and dexterity in gymnastics.

1. ☐ Introduced and understood
   ☐ Performs basic skill
   ☐ Conditioned response with variations

2. ☐ Introduced and understood
   ☐ Performs basic skill
   ☐ Conditioned response with variations

3. ☐ Introduced and understood
   ☐ Performs basic skill
   ☐ Conditioned response with variations

1. Back Rocker

DESCRIPTION:
   Sit with length of mat behind, hands beside hips, knees bent. Then lean back and raise legs overhead. Allow legs to fall in front of body and rock up to sitting position.

VARIATIONS:
   Can you rock back with arms held out sideward like wings?
   Can you hold arms above your head as you rock back?
   Can you touch the mat over your head with your hands?
   Can you cross your legs at the ankles when you rock?
   Can you grab your ankles with your hands and pull as you rock?
   Who can make their legs straight at the top of the rock?
   Who can straddle their legs at the top?
   Who can touch the mat over their head with one toe? With both toes?

2. Back Balance

DESCRIPTION:

Sit with knees bent and hands on mat. Rock back, raise legs overhead, and balance there.

VARIATIONS:

Can you hold your feet there for ten counts?

Can you straighten one knee? The other knee?

Can you hold both legs straight? Both legs bent?

Can you touch one knee to your shoulder?

Can you pretend to ride a bicycle while you are upside down?

Who can take long walking steps with their legs?

Can you touch the floor over your head with one toe?

3. Back Rocker to Puppy Dog

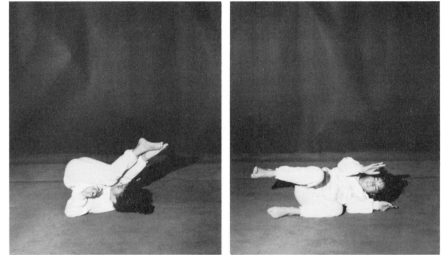

DESCRIPTION:

Start from sitting, knees bent, and rock back with arms raised overhead. Allow legs to fall to one side keeping knees bent and roll over legs to *puppy dog position* on knees and forearms.

VARIATIONS:

Can you hold the *back balance* for ten counts before rolling out?

Can you roll out immediately as you rock back?

Who can fall to a different side?

Who can do another *puppy dog roll* right after they land from the first one?

Novice Springboard Activities

Forward Bouncing

The springboard offers children that magic moment of floating in the air, free of the grip of gravity. To be sure, it is a short moment, but there is much stimulation of the inner ear and, especially, proprioceptors in the legs, which find themselves without the pressure of gravity. The eyes and the ears and the kinesthetic receptors are brought into full use to prepare the body for the landing.

Very young children can be apprehensive about having both feet off the floor at the same time. Do not rush them. Give children many opportunities and allow them to step off with one foot as long as they show concern.

The landing becomes very important when the performer finally is willing to jump upward into the air.

Caution: Emphasize landing with the knees bent out over the toes and the waist bent to lean the shoulders out over the toes.

1. ☐ Introduced and understood
☐ Performs basic skill
☐ Conditioned response with variations

2. ☐ Introduced and understood
☐ Performs basic skill
☐ Conditioned response with variations

3. ☐ Introduced and understood
☐ Performs basic skill
☐ Conditioned response with variations

1. Jump Off

CAUTION:

Before beginning springboard activities every child should practice the *balanced landing position*. Knees are slightly bent, hips are slightly bent, and arms are stretched forward and outward. Children should jump from the floor and land with this posture many times before getting on the springboard.

DESCRIPTION:

Start standing on board with toes near forward edge. Push against board and jump into air and off board. Finish in *landing position*.

VARIATIONS:

Can you hold the landing three counts without taking a step?
Can you land with your feet close together?
Can you land with your feet apart?
Can you leap onto the board and bounce off?

2. Knee Slapper

DESCRIPTION:

Bounce off end of board and slap knees at top of bounce. Finish in *landing position.*

TEACHER'S NOTE:

Children should lift knees quickly so as to complete the *knee slapper* on the way upward, thus leaving the body free to prepare for the landing as it is coming down.

VARIATIONS:

Can you hit both knees at once?

Can you slap your knees twice?

Can you cross your arms and slap your knees?

Do you hit the board on its most bouncy spot?

Where is the most bouncy spot?

3. Seat Kicker

DESCRIPTION:

Bounce off end of board and quickly bend knees so heels come up near buttocks. Finish in *landing position.*

VARIATIONS:

Can you hold the *landing position* for three counts?

Can you raise your arms upward to get more height?

Can you bounce a little farther out from the board?

Can you land on a target and hold your balance? A small mat (about 1½ feet square) is an excellent target for the landing (it must be nonslip).

Can you bounce over a soft obstacle? (A loosely held ribbon or rope makes a good obstacle.)

Twisting

Twisting involves turning the angle of the shoulders with respect to the hips. In Developmental Gymnastics most of the twisting movements have a very slight change of angle and thus often look more like turning movements than twisting. Nevertheless, these activities involve inner ear stimulation and orientation in space that is very important to full kinesensory development.

1.
- ☐ Introduced and understood
- ☐ Performs basic skill
- ☐ Conditioned response with variations

2.
- ☐ Introduced and understood
- ☐ Performs basic skill
- ☐ Conditioned response with variations

3.
- ☐ Introduced and understood
- ☐ Performs basic skill
- ☐ Conditioned response with variations

1. Bouncing Up

DESCRIPTION:

Stand on springboard. Start bouncing and bounce several times. Then bounce off and land *on balance.*

NOTE:

There is no twisting in this movement, which is designed to prepare the performer to get more time and height in the air.

VARIATIONS:

Can you bounce off on the third bounce?
Can you bounce off on the sixth bounce?
Can you hold your landing for five counts?
Who can land on the target?
Can you bounce with your arms held like wings?
Can you bounce with your arms on your hips?

2. Bounce and Turn

3. Around and Back

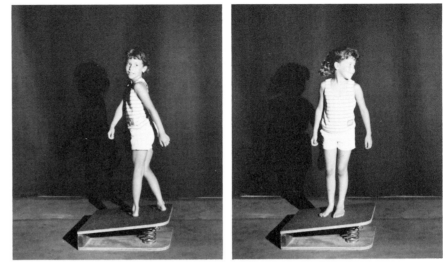

DESCRIPTION:

Stand on springboard facing straight ahead. Start bouncing and, as you are bouncing, gradually turn until you have turned all the way around. Then bounce off and land *on balance.*

VARIATIONS:

Can you hold your arms out wide?
Can you hold your arms close to your body?
Can you hold your hands on top of your head?
Can you hold a ball in your hands?
Can you do a variation of your own?

DESCRIPTION:

Stand on springboard facing straight ahead. Bounce until a complete turn is finished; then without stopping do another complete turn in the opposite direction. Bounce off and finish in *landing position.*

VARIATIONS:

How many bounces does it take you? Eight? Six? Four?
Does it make you dizzy?
Can you hold your arms stretched outward?
Can you hold your hands on top of your head?
Can you hold your hands on your hips?
Can you finish with a *seat kicker?*
What other variation can you do?

Rolling Sequence

When young children are asked to execute more than one skill in a series they are required to exhibit serial memory. This ability takes time to develop and should not be expected from the beginning. Practice on these skills in series will stimulate the mind and will assist children in the development of serial memory.

1.
☐ Introduced and understood
☐ Performs basic skill
☐ Conditioned response with variations

2.
☐ Introduced and understood
☐ Performs basic skill
☐ Conditioned response with variations

3.
☐ Introduced and understood
☐ Performs basic skill
☐ Conditioned response with variations

1. Land, Then Squat

DESCRIPTION:
Bounce off end of springboard; after landing bend knees and squat so that hands touch mat.

VARIATIONS:
Can you put your hands close together?
Can you put your hands wide apart? Both to one side? Where do you balance best?
Can you bounce farther before you land and squat?
Can you hold your landing balance for three counts, then squat?

2. Land, Then Bunny Hop

DESCRIPTION:

Bounce off end of springboard; after landing, squat, reach out, and take all the weight on both arms while pulling both feet up closer to hands. The alternate reaching of both hands followed by bringing up both feet is called the *bunny hop*.

VARIATIONS:

Can the bunny take small hops?

Can the bunny take big hops?

Can you lift your feet off the mat when you hop?

Who can do the *lame dog walk* after landing? The *bear walk?*

3. Land—Bunny Hop—Tip Over

DESCRIPTION:

Bounce off springboard; after landing, squat, do *bunny hop*, then look behind and *tip over*.

VARIATIONS:

Can you take two hops before doing the *tip over?*

Can you take three hops before doing the *tip over?*

Can you do the *lame dog walk* after landing?

Can you do the *bear walk?*

With Table

There is a certain sensation and feeling of accomplishment in bouncing off the springboard onto a higher surface. Ensure that the higher surface (tumbling table) is stable.

Prerequisite: Children must have mastered the novice level forward bouncing and twisting before attempting these movements. The close edge of the table could easily trip a very small child who was not very well prepared. Have children *step* up onto the table and jump off before they bounce up onto the table.

Caution: It is very important to assist children down from the table until the child has shown the ability to negotiate the jump.

Note: Determine the distance of the board from the table by observing children bounce off the board onto the mats and notice the trajectory.

1.
☐ Introduced and understood
☐ Performs basic skill
☐ Conditioned response with variations

2.
☐ Introduced and understood
☐ Performs basic skill
☐ Conditioned response with variations

3.
☐ Introduced and understood
☐ Performs basic skill
☐ Conditioned response with variations

1. Land On—Jump Off

DESCRIPTION:

Springboard should be about 8 inches from end of tumbling table, depending upon the size and experience of the child. Bounce off springboard and land on tumbling table. Then jump off table. Finish in *landing position.*

VARIATIONS:

Can you land in the center of the table?
Can you balance on the table when you land?
Can you step up onto the table?
From standing on the table can you squat down, place your hands on the table, and bounce your feet up and off the table?

2. Land On—Knee Slapper Off

DESCRIPTION:

With springboard about 8 inches from end of tumbling table, bounce up onto table. Then move close to forward edge of table, execute *knee slapper*, and land on mat below. Finish in *landing position*.

VARIATIONS:

Can you land on a target?

Can you balance when you land?

Can you land on balance when you bounce to the table?

Can you slap your knees between the springboard and the table?

3. Land On—Seat Kicker Off

DESCRIPTION:

With springboard about 8 inches from end of tumbling table, bounce up onto table. Then move to edge of table, execute *seat kicker*, and land on mat below. Finish in *landing position*.

VARIATIONS:

Can you hold your arms out wide like the wings of a plane when you jump off the table?

Can you hold your balance when you land on the table? On the mat after the table?

Can you land on a target?

Can you do a *seat kicker* between springboard and table, then another between table and mat?

Novice Low Horizontal Bar Activities

Swinging Under

The low horizontal bar provides children the opportunity for certain sensory, muscle, and reflex development that is not available from other apparatus. When children work on the horizontal bar the support goes through the arms and shoulders to the bar, rather than through the legs to the floor. Thus, hanging and swinging with a new kinesthetic point of support provides a new type of arm, shoulder, and abdomen development as well as the new types of sensory development required to allow for the support coming through the arms. If adjustable, the bar should be set just a little lower than chest high. This will allow children to jump to a support position with their feet free of the floor.

1. ☐ Introduced and understood
   ☐ Performs basic skill
   ☐ Conditioned response with variations

2. ☐ Introduced and understood
   ☐ Performs basic skill
   ☐ Conditioned response with variations

3. ☐ Introduced and understood
   ☐ Performs basic skill
   ☐ Conditioned response with variations

1. Hang and Swing

DESCRIPTION:
Sit under bar with buttocks in line with supports, knees bent, and feet on mat. Reach up and take hold of bar, leave arms straight, lift hips off mat to hanging position. Now swing shoulders back and forth under bar by pushing knees out over feet. Finish by lowering buttocks to mat in sitting position.

VARIATIONS:
Can you look at your hands?
Can you look at your knees?
Can you swing your shoulders in a circular motion?
Can you swing your shoulders from side to side?
Can you slide one hand over near the other, then slide it back?
Can you slide one hand at a time until you move across the bar?
Can you move your feet to one side, then the other?
Can you turn around to face the opposite direction?

2. Hang and Walk

3. Back Up to Standing

DESCRIPTION:

Sit under bar with buttocks in line with supports, knees bent, feet on mat. Take hold of bar with hands; leaving arms straight lift buttocks off mat. Now take a few small steps forward, then a few backward to create a swinging action.

VARIATIONS:

Can you walk forward and backward three times?

Can you look at your knees as you swing?

Can you look at the bar as you swing?

Can you take very short steps?

Can you take giant steps?

DESCRIPTION:

Sit on mat under bar and take hold of bar with hands. Lift hips off mat and swing back and forth by taking steps with feet. On the way backward push hard with feet and push down with hands until you rise up to a standing position.

VARIATIONS:

Can you make it all the way to standing?

Can you swing so far forward that the back swing carries you right up in a smooth action?

Can you keep your arms straight when you rise up backward?

Can you swing so far forward that your ears come between your arms?

Support above Bar

Supporting the weight above the bar is a new experience for most young children. Prepare children by having them feel arm support on the floor with such activities as the *scamper* and *leg lifter.* If this *front support* on the floor is done just a few seconds before getting on the bar, the necessary muscle nerves will be stimulated and the chance of success is greatly improved.

Teacher's Note: Among gymnasts there is much discussion about which grip is best, having the palms facing the performer (*double under grip*) or having the palms facing away from the performer (*double over grip*). In some cases the description will tell you what grip is to be used. If no mention is made of the grip, either grip is satisfactory. By and large, in Developmental Gymnastic movements either grip is safe. Slipping can be caused by a wet palm. If a child complains of slipping, you should provide a towel to wipe the hands and the bar.

1.
☐ Introduced and understood
☐ Performs basic skill
☐ Conditioned response with variations

2.
☐ Introduced and understood
☐ Performs basic skill
☐ Conditioned response with variations

3.
☐ Introduced and understood
☐ Performs basic skill
☐ Conditioned response with variations

1. Front Support

DESCRIPTION:
Stand facing bar with hands on bar as wide as hips. Jump up and support weight on arms.

VARIATIONS:
Can you see your toes?
Can you look up and see the ceiling without losing your balance?
Can you hold your balance for three counts? Ten counts?
Can you turn your shoulders so that they face one side, then the other?

2. Space Walk

DESCRIPTION:

While in *front support*, "walk" by swinging the legs in opposite directions.

VARIATIONS:

Can you take long steps?

Can you take short fast steps?

Can you swish your feet like scissors?

Can you pretend to pedal a bicycle?

Can you tuck both knees up under the bar at the same time?

3. Knee Bender

CAUTION:

Very young children, if they should fall forward, may let go of the bar since their reflexes are to reach for the floor rather than hold onto the bar. The teacher should stand in front of the bar and ensure that the child does not fall forward during the first three or four attempts at this movement.

DESCRIPTION

While in *front support*, bend knees so that heels come up behind.

VARIATIONS:

Can you hold for three counts?

Can you drop your feet down and then bring them back to the bent position?

Grip Changes and Turning

This sequence of activities provides the children with the opportunity to experience different grips on the bar and thus a different feeling in the forearms and hands. These activities also give children a wider range of skills at the novice level of difficulty and will thus make them better prepared for the intermediate and advanced programs.

1.
☐ Introduced and understood
☐ Performs basic skill
☐ Conditioned response with variations

2.
☐ Introduced and understood
☐ Performs basic skill
☐ Conditioned response with variations

3.
☐ Introduced and understood
☐ Performs basic skill
☐ Conditioned response with variations

1. Over Grip Hand Walk

DESCRIPTION:

Sit under bar with buttocks in line with supports. Reach up and take bar with fingers over bar and thumbs on inside toward each other. This is called the *double over grip.* Keeping arms straight, lift hips off mat and then slide one hand to the other. Slide the other hand away and continue sliding until you "walk" across the length of the bar.

VARIATIONS:

Can you slide by taking very small steps?
Can you take slow steps? A little faster? How fast can you go?
Can you take longer steps?

2. Mixed Grip Hand Walk

DESCRIPTION:

Sit under bar and face directly toward one of the supports with knees bent and feet on floor. Reach up and grab bar with both hands, palms facing in opposite directions. This is called the *mixed grip.* Now lift hips off mat and walk hands down length of bar. Sit down to finish.

VARIATIONS:

Can you take very small steps?

Can you take larger steps?

Can you slide the leading hand forward, then the trailing hand forward?

3. Turning in a Circle

DESCRIPTION:

Sit under bar, reach up and grab bar with both hands, and lift hips off mat. Now walk feet around to one side and change your grip to a *mixed grip.* Continue walking feet in a circle and change grip when necessary to maintain a strong support.

VARIATIONS:

Can you turn slowly?

Can you turn a little faster?

Can you turn in the opposite direction?

Can you turn around in a circle, then back in the opposite direction?

Around the Bar

This sequence of skills is to prepare children to rotate around the bar with the bar tucked into the bend of the hip. The sequence begins with the *front support,* which is so important that it appears three times in the novice program. Like the *back rocker* on the mats, the *front support* is a fundamental posture from which many other activities begin. It should be mastered along with many variations to the point of a conditioned response.

1. ☐ Introduced and understood
   ☐ Performs basic skill
   ☐ Conditioned response with variations

2. ☐ Introduced and understood
   ☐ Performs basic skill
   ☐ Conditioned response with variations

3. ☐ Introduced and understood
   ☐ Performs basic skill
   ☐ Conditioned response with variations

1. Front Support

DESCRIPTION:
    Place hands on bar wide enough apart so that hips will just fit between them. Jump onto bar and balance with arms straight.

VARIATIONS:
    Can you hold your body straight and tight?
    Can you lift one knee and then the other?
    Can you point your toes downward?
    Can you swing your feet from side to side?
    Can you spread your feet and legs apart and bring them back together?
    Can you alternately touch toes, then heels?

2. Hip Hug

CAUTION:

The teacher should stand in front of the performer the first few times to ensure that very young children do not fall forward.

DESCRIPTION:

Take *front support* position on bar. Place bar in bend of hips and lean slightly forward as you raise both knees and hug bar between legs and abdomen.

TEACHER'S NOTE:

Where the bar touches the legs while in the *front support* can be adjusted by a slight bend in the arms and by pushing the shoulders either up or down. It is sometimes difficult for a child to get the bar into the bend of the hips, but practice will help find the right kinesthetic feeling.

VARIATIONS:

Can you feel the bar at the hips? Can you slowly go from the *hip hug* back to the *front support* without losing balance?

Can you alternate from hug to support several times?

3. Bar Hang

CAUTION:

About one in thirty children cannot do the *bar hang* without letting go of the bar to reach for the mat. This is a reflex action, which can be overcome only by developing confidence in the bar as a source of support. The teacher should hold each child at the shoulder, being sure that every child has confidence in the bar as a source of support.

DESCRIPTION:

Jump to *front support*, hug bar with hips, and lean forward until body is hanging at hips. Hands do not release from bar. To recover, straighten legs and pull bar slightly up abdomen. Return to *front support*.

TEACHER'S NOTE:

Most children will need a lift at the shoulders to return to *front support* position.

VARIATIONS:

Can you return to the *front support* by yourself?

Can you look at your knees? At the floor?

Rotating under the Bar

This sequence involves the rotation of the body while suspended by the arms. Grip is very important and children must have confidence in their ability to hang by their hands. If children complain that the bar is slick, the teacher should wipe the bar and the child's hands with a dry towel. Some children will perspire in the palms when others will not, so it is very possible that one child feels the bar to be slick while another child does not.

1.
☐ Introduced and understood
☐ Performs basic skill
☐ Conditioned response with variations

2.
☐ Introduced and understood
☐ Performs basic skill
☐ Conditioned response with variations

3.
☐ Introduced and understood
☐ Performs basic skill
☐ Conditioned response with variations

1. Toe Touch

DESCRIPTION:
Hang below bar; bring one leg up so that toe touches bar.

VARIATIONS:
Can you hook your toe under the bar?
Can you touch the other toe?
Can you touch both toes?
Can you touch your knee to your chest?
Can you alternately kick one foot upward in front while hanging, then the other?

2. Knee to Chest

DESCRIPTION:

Hang below bar, bring one knee to chest, then return to mat and bring other knee to chest.

VARIATIONS:

Can you look at the knee?

Can you pull the knee close to your chest?

Can you bring the opposite knee to your chest?

Can you alternate them quickly?

Can you bring both knees to your chest?

3. Bat Hang

DESCRIPTION:

Hang below bar, bring both knees to chest, and continue pulling knees between arms by lifting hips until you are hanging upside down.

TEACHER'S NOTE:

It is easier for most children to bring one knee up and push off with the other foot. The supporting foot then follows.

VARIATIONS:

Can you look at your knees while you hang?

Can you look back at the wall behind you?

Can you look at your stomach?

Can you come down and go right back up?

Hip Casting

Casting away from the bar helps to develop strength and confidence in the arms as well as body awareness. Much of the action occurs from the bending and arching of the hip.

Now for the third time, we include the *front support.* It is important that the performer gain awareness and control of all other muscles in the body. Therefore, movements of the shoulders, arms, and toes should be included along with the usual movements of the legs. In the *cast away* we now use that point on the hips where bending occurs. By swinging the lower portion of the body under the bar and leaning the upper portion over the bar, the performer comes toward a *pike position.* Then the action of pushing against the bar with the hips and forcefully lifting the legs backward will raise the body off the bar. It is important at this point to learn just how much forward lean the shoulders should have in order to keep some of the weight on the arms.

1.
- ☐ Introduced and understood
- ☐ Performs basic skill
- ☐ Conditioned response with variations

2.
- ☐ Introduced and understood
- ☐ Performs basic skill
- ☐ Conditioned response with variations

3.
- ☐ Introduced and understood
- ☐ Performs basic skill
- ☐ Conditioned response with variations

1. Front Support

DESCRIPTION:
Stand before bar with *double over grip,* hands spread no wider than hips. Jump up to a support with most of weight on arms.

VARIATIONS:
Can you hold your legs straight and together?
Can you hold your body tight and motionless?
Can you swing your toes from side to side?
Can you lift and lower your knees?
Can you push the bar downward to touch the thighs?
When you drop down from the bar can you hold your balance with hands still on the bar? Are your arms slightly bent? They should be.
How far from the bar are your feet? Not quite an arm's length is about right.

2. Double Leg Swing

DESCRIPTION:

While in *front support,* hold legs together and swing both legs slightly forward and slightly backward. Simultaneously counteract tendency to be pulled backward off bar by leaning shoulders slightly forward as feet come forward.

VARIATIONS:

Can you swing smoothly without being pulled off the bar?

Can you swing your toes forward two times? Three times?

Does your body get pulled backward? To counteract that backward pull, lean forward with the shoulders a little bit.

Can you take a little bit bigger swing with the toes?

Can you look at your toes when they swing forward?

3. Cast Away

DESCRIPTION:

While in *front support* allow legs to swing together, first forward, then backward, then forward again. On second swing backward raise legs extra high so that hips come off bar. Then allow body to come to a *landing position* on mat so that grip on bar can be held for balance.

VARIATIONS:

Does the extra preparatory swing help you get higher?

Can you pause a moment in the air before falling to the mat?

Can you land *on balance?*

Can you land with your hands still holding to the bar?

Can you push away and land on the mat without holding to the bar?

Can you bend your knees as your legs swing backward?

Novice Tumbling Table/Wedge Activities

Vaulting Over

The tumbling table is a great learning environment. In the form of a block, it provides a surface, like a couch or hassock, that children can climb onto and jump from. Further, it offers an easy introduction to activities that require placing weight onto the arms. In the form of a wedge, it provides a sloping surface that children can roll down or up. Many children will be successful doing the *tip over* from the tumbling table long before they are successful on the level mat.

1.
- ☐ Introduced and understood
- ☐ Performs basic skill
- ☐ Conditioned response with variations

2.
- ☐ Introduced and understood
- ☐ Performs basic skill
- ☐ Conditioned response with variations

3.
- ☐ Introduced and understood
- ☐ Performs basic skill
- ☐ Conditioned response with variations

1. Crawl

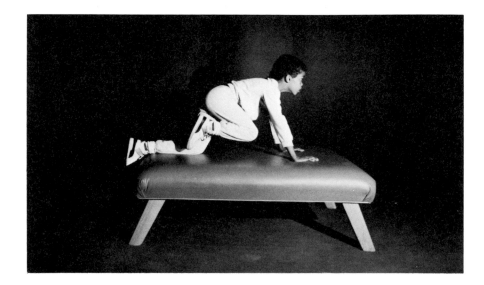

DESCRIPTION:
Climb onto table on hands and knees. Crawl across table and turn near far edge so as to reach down to mat with legs to get off table.

VARIATIONS:
Can you turn around and get down safely?
Can you turn in a circle on top of the table?
Can you crawl sideways?
As you prepare to get off, can you bounce your knees up and bring both feet off together?

2. Scamper

DESCRIPTION:

Climb onto table on hands and feet (knees do not touch on the *scamper*). Scamper across table and turn to get off safely at far edge.

VARIATIONS:

Can you carefully get down so as not to fall or lose your balance?

Can you scamper sideways?

Can you turn in a circle in the middle of the table?

As you prepare to get off the far end of the table, can you bounce your feet so that both feet come off at the same time?

3. Side Bunny Hop

DESCRIPTION:

Stand with table to your side. Place hands on table and hop with both feet at the same time onto table in a *hands-and-feet position*. Hop first with hands and then with feet until you reach far edge of table; then bounce feet up and over the edge and down to mat.

VARIATIONS:

Can you keep your feet together as though you had just one big foot?

Can you turn to place the table on your opposite side?

Can you hop across the table and then hop back across in the opposite direction?

Rolling Forward

These rolling activities are among the most motivating skills in Developmental Gymnastics for young children. The inner ear stimulation of rolling over and over is very beneficial and a great deal of fun for the children. Have children roll for awhile to the left and then for awhile to the right. Both directions are important for balanced development.

The tumbling table offers children the easiest way to tip hips over head in a safe manner. Children can learn the *tip over* on the tumbling table at the novice level, and this action and skill can later be transferred to the mats at the intermediate level.

1. ☐ Introduced and understood
   ☐ Performs basic skill
   ☐ Conditioned response with variations

2. ☐ Introduced and understood
   ☐ Performs basic skill
   ☐ Conditioned response with variations

3. ☐ Introduced and understood
   ☐ Performs basic skill
   ☐ Conditioned response with variations

1. Log Roll

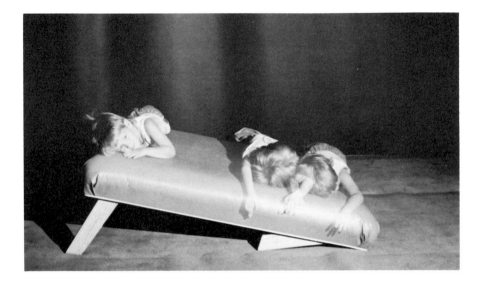

DESCRIPTION:
Lie on stomach at high end of slanted table with arms up to protect face. Roll like a log down to bottom.

VARIATIONS:
Can you roll slowly down the hill?
Can you roll faster down the hill?
Do you keep rolling after you reach the mat?
Can you lie facing the opposite direction?

2. Puppy Dog Roll

DESCRIPTION:

Start on hands and knees at high end of slanted table. From *all-fours position* sit back so that seat touches heels and bring elbows and forearms to mat in front of body. Body is now in the *puppy dog position* with head down and back rounded. Lean down the incline, catching body with hip, then shoulder, and roll across back and return to *puppy dog position.*

VARIATIONS:

Do you roll smoothly over your back?
Do you keep your knees tucked up even while you roll?
Can you finish on your hands and knees?
Can you face the opposite direction?

3. Tip Over

DESCRIPTION:

Crawl up slanted table on hands and knees until knees are right at edge of table. Place hands on mat. Place head on mat between hands, tuck chin under, and push off with knees to tip hips over head. Finish in sitting position.

VARIATIONS:

Can you roll smoothly?
Can you look back up between your legs before you tip over?
Can you finish with your legs straight?
Can you finish with your legs crossed?
Can you finish with your knees bent?

Rolling Backward

Rolling backward over the head requires a number of strengths and prerequisite skills. Children should not actually turn over their head backward at the novice level. The head is large compared to the body and the possibility of neck injury should be avoided. Therefore, the novice level skills are preparatory only.

1. ☐ Introduced and understood
   ☐ Performs basic skill
   ☐ Conditioned response with variations

2. ☐ Introduced and understood
   ☐ Performs basic skill
   ☐ Conditioned response with variations

3. ☐ Introduced and understood
   ☐ Performs basic skill
   ☐ Conditioned response with variations

1. Seat Balance

DESCRIPTION:
Sit on slanted table with high end to your back. Raise legs and feet to balance on seat.

VARIATIONS:
Can you hold your legs straight?
Can you hold your legs a little higher?
Can you reach up and touch your legs with your hands?

2. Back Rocker

DESCRIPTION:

Sit on slanted table with high end to your back. Rock backward and pull legs and feet up over head.

VARIATIONS:

Can you rock your feet a little farther back over your head?

As you come forward from the *back rocker* can you pull your heels in close to your seat? Does this raise your seat off the table?

As you come forward can you put both knees on the same side of the mat and rise to a *knee stand?*

3. Toe Touch

DESCRIPTION:

Sit on mat with tumbling table far enough behind you that you can do a *back rocker* without touching table with your head. Then rock backward and bring your feet over your head to touch table behind you.

VARIATIONS:

Can you touch the table with one foot?

Can you touch with the other foot?

Can you balance and touch with one foot and then the other?

Can you touch with both feet at the same time?

Novice Beam Activities

Balancing on the Level Beam 1. Step On and Over

The beam will develop balance and requires improved kinesthetic senses not only in the legs but also throughout the body. Almost every skill described for the beam can be practiced on a line on the floor.

Caution: For very young children who are not yet secure with their control of running, jumping, and negotiating stairs, it is best to learn these activities on a line on the floor and/or a very low beam. All novice activities should be performed on a beam that is below the level of the knees, preferably within 6 inches of the floor.

Teacher's Note: Children should always be allowed to place their eyes at the most advantageous angle. Looking down at the feet may cause one to lose the sense of the horizon, yet looking up at the horizon may cause the unexperienced person to lose a sense of the location of the beam. Some point lower than the horizon but that allows the child to see the beam will usually provide the most advantageous visual field for the development of balance on the beam.

1.
- ☐ Introduced and understood
- ☐ Performs basic skill
- ☐ Conditioned response with variations

2.
- ☐ Introduced and understood
- ☐ Performs basic skill
- ☐ Conditioned response with variations

3.
- ☐ Introduced and understood
- ☐ Performs basic skill
- ☐ Conditioned response with variations

TEACHER'S NOTE:
The beam should be very low to the floor and definitely below the level of the knees on all novice activities.

DESCRIPTION:
Face beam. Put one foot on; then push up and over, landing on other side in *balanced landing position.*

VARIATIONS:
Can you make a safe and balanced landing?
Can you push off with the opposite foot?
How high can you go?
How far can you go?

2. Balance On

DESCRIPTION:

Face low beam. Step up and balance in standing position.

VARIATIONS:

Can you balance for three counts? Six counts?

Can you jump onto the beam and catch your balance?

Can you balance on one foot?

Can you turn around?

IMAGERY:

You are at the edge of a river in the jungle. A log floats by and you step onto the log to get to the other side of the river. Now the river is wider and you must catch a log and ride it down the river for a while before you jump off. Now you are riding a log down the river and you come to a bridge and must duck down. Now you see an alligator on the bank in front of you so you turn around to get off on the opposite bank. Ah, safe at last.

3. Step to the Side

DESCRIPTION:

Balance standing sideways to beam with feet about a shoulder's width apart. Lean more on one foot than the other. Then lean the other way. Then lean again and slide free foot toward supporting foot.

VARIATIONS:

Can you take a small step and still keep your balance?

Can you go back to where you were?

Can you take a larger step?

IMAGERY:

You are riding a log down the river. You find that you are standing on a knot and must move to one side. Now you find that there is mud on your shoes that makes your feet slippery, so one foot at a time you must wipe the mud off. Then it starts to rain and you must hold both hands against your forehead to keep rain out of your eyes. Then the log goes into some low-hanging trees and you must use one hand to push the branches aside. Ah, safe at last.

Vaulting on the Level Beam

Vaulting activities require the use of the arms for a part of the body support. Children learn to lean onto the arms and develop some ability to maneuver while supported by the arms.

1.
☐ Introduced and understood
☐ Performs basic skill
☐ Conditioned response with variations

2.
☐ Introduced and understood
☐ Performs basic skill
☐ Conditioned response with variations

3.
☐ Introduced and understood
☐ Performs basic skill
☐ Conditioned response with variations

1. Front Support

DESCRIPTION:

Take *hands-and-knees position* facing low level beam. Reach up and place hands on beam, then raise knees off floor. This is the *front support position.*

VARIATIONS:

Can you raise one hand off the beam?
Can you march with your hands?
Can you raise one foot off the floor?
Can you raise your feet alternately as in marching?
Can you bounce both feet off the floor?
Can you bounce your feet up and do a *seat kicker?*
Can you bounce your feet up and do a *straddle?*

2. Sidewinder

DESCRIPTION:

Stand facing sideways to low beam. Reach down and place hands on beam and move feet back until weight is equally distributed between arms and feet. Now one hand at a time step sideways, and one foot at a time bring feet back in line with hands.

VARIATIONS:

Can you start at the middle of the beam and sidewind to the end?

Can you go in the opposite direction?

Can you move very slowly? Can you go a little faster?

Can you put your feet a little farther from the beam?

Can you bounce on both feet as though they were one?

3. Dancing Crab

DESCRIPTION:

Sit on beam, place hands beside hips, and put feet on floor. Then raise hips off beam to become supported by hands on beam and feet on floor. This is the *crab position.* Now alternately raise one foot, then the other, as though the crab is dancing.

VARIATIONS:

Can you raise your foot high in front of you?

Can you raise your knees high?

Can you raise your feet so high that your legs become straight?

Can you bounce twice on one foot, then twice on the other?

Can you raise one foot, then the hand on the same side of the body?

Can you raise one foot, then the hand on the opposite side of the body?

Balancing on the Slanted Beam

The slanted beam provides the opportunity for gradual increase in height above the mat. A mark should be put on the beam at a height from which the children are used to jumping (approximately 8 to 12 inches for 3 year olds, 10 to 16 inches for 4 and 5 year olds). These marks can then be used as instructional guides.

Caution: Since children will be jumping off the beam to land on the mat, they should have previously mastered the novice level of upright agility on the mats as well as falling and landing.

1. ☐ Introduced and understood
   ☐ Performs basic skill
   ☐ Conditioned response with variations

2. ☐ Introduced and understood
   ☐ Performs basic skill
   ☐ Conditioned response with variations

3. ☐ Introduced and understood
   ☐ Performs basic skill
   ☐ Conditioned response with variations

1. Walk to First Mark

DESCRIPTION:
Stand at low end of slanted beam facing toward the high end. Step carefully onto beam and walk upward to first mark. Turn and jump down to recover in *balanced landing position.*

VARIATIONS:
Can you walk very slowly?
Can you hold your arms out wide?
Can you hold your arms on your hips?
Can you hold your balance when you jump down to the mat?
Who can hold their hands on top of their head?

2. Slide to First Mark

DESCRIPTION:

Stand at low end of slanted beam facing beam. Step on with both feet so that you are standing sideways to beam. Step sideways with uphill foot; then slide other foot up to meet it. Continue step sliding until you reach the first mark. Jump down to *balanced landing position.*

VARIATIONS:

Who can take very small side steps? Who can take larger steps?

Who can hold their arms out wide for balance?

Who can hold their hands on top of their head?

Who can turn around and lead with the opposite foot?

3. Go Backward to First Mark

DESCRIPTION:

Stand at low end of slanted beam with high end to your back. Stand on beam with both feet, one foot behind the other. Now carefully and slowly go backward up slanted beam until you get to first mark. Then turn to the side and jump down to *balanced landing position.*

TEACHER'S NOTE:

This activity is not called "walking" backward because the inexperienced child may not feel secure enough to take one foot off the beam. Most children will "go" backward by sliding the rear foot and then sliding the front foot back to meet it. This is perfectly all right.

VARIATIONS:

Can you feel the beam behind you with your foot as you slide it backward?

Can you stay on balance as you go backward?

Can you hold your arms out wide for balance?

Vaulting on the Slanted Beam

Vaulting the beam is like vaulting a fence. These novice activities are preparing the hand and foot patterns for a smooth front vault and a smooth rear vault at the higher levels of difficulty.

1.
☐ Introduced and understood
☐ Performs basic skill
☐ Conditioned response with variations

2.
☐ Introduced and understood
☐ Performs basic skill
☐ Conditioned response with variations

3.
☐ Introduced and understood
☐ Performs basic skill
☐ Conditioned response with variations

1. Bear Dance

DESCRIPTION:

Stand straddling slanted beam at low end facing high end. Reach out and place hands on beam; spread feet to *straddle position*. Now execute *straddle switch* with feet. This is the *bear dance*.

VARIATIONS:

How high can you raise each foot?
Can you pause for a moment with your foot in the air?
Can you wave to other bears with the foot that is in the air?
Can you dance fast? Can you dance very slowly?

2. Bear Bounce

3. Turning Toy

DESCRIPTION:

Stand straddling slanted beam at low end facing high end. Lean forward and place hands on beam. With feet straddled bounce hips upward and bring feet closer to hands. Reach out with hands and then bounce hips and feet again. Take about four bounces and then turn off the beam to *balanced landing position.*

VARIATIONS:

Can you keep your feet straddled as you bounce your hips upward?

How high can you bounce your hips?

Do you feel that your arms can support your weight? Do you keep your arms straight and tight?

DESCRIPTION:

Stand straddle of slanted beam at low end facing high end. Now alternately lift feet sideways with legs straight like a toy to execute a standing *straddle switch.* Then lean on one foot, bring the other foot up and behind, and do a one-half turn to bring yourself away from beam still standing in a *straddle position.*

VARIATIONS:

Can you continue turning to make a second turn?

Can you stand beside the beam in a *straddle position,* then turn onto the beam and then off on the other side?

Can you hold your arms out wide like a robot?

3. Intermediate Program:

Students in Grades 2 and 3 Who Have Completed the Novice Program

Intermediate Mat Activities

Upright Balance

Balancing activities challenge the reflex system and help to make the body more responsive to the inner ear and other proprioceptive sensors. There is also some strength development in the supporting member and some range of motion development in the members used for ballast.

Under some conditions, when there is no danger of injury, it will make the performer more aware of the kinesthetic system to execute the balance positions with the eyes closed. Cutting out the visual system places more complete dependence upon the *feelings of movement* that come from the various sensory receptors in the muscles, tendons, joints, and inner ear.

4.
- ☐ Introduced and understood
- ☐ Performs basic skill
- ☐ Conditioned response with variations

5.
- ☐ Introduced and understood
- ☐ Performs basic skill
- ☐ Conditioned response with variations

6.
- ☐ Introduced and understood
- ☐ Performs basic skill
- ☐ Conditioned response with variations

4. V-Seat

DESCRIPTION:

From sitting with knees together and bent, raise legs upward and straighten legs at knees to balance on buttocks.

VARIATIONS:

Can you point your toes outward away from the body?

Who can take their hands off the floor?

Who can reach forward with the hands and touch their shins? Their toes?

Can you hold your arms out sideways like wings?

Can you scissor your legs back and forth? Who can cross their legs?

Can you hold your legs in a *straddle?*

Can you bend just one leg and keep the other one straight?

Can you hold the *V-seat* for six counts with your eyes closed?

Who can hold the *V-seat* very still and then move only their fingers?

5. Front Support Balance

DESCRIPTION:

From hands and knees on mat, press down against mat with toes, raise knees off mat to take *all-fours position.*

VARIATIONS:

Can you raise one hand off the mat? The other hand? Alternate?

Can you touch the opposite shoulder with the free hand? Alternate?

Can you make a four-count movement by (1) touching the shoulder, (2) extending the arm outward, (3) touching the shoulder, (4) returning to the *all-fours position?* Alternate arms two times each.

Can you raise one foot off the mat? The other foot?

Can you take small walking steps without hands, two out, two back?

Can you balance by raising one hand and the foot on the same side? The foot on the opposite side?

Can you straighten and stiffen your body until it is straight like a board?

6. One-Foot Balance

DESCRIPTION:

Stand tall and erect. Hold arms outward slightly for ballast; then raise one foot behind you to balance on one foot only.

VARIATIONS:

Can you hold your balance for ten counts?

Can you hold very still while you balance?

Take a big breath and let it out slowly while you are balancing.

Who can hold their free foot out to the side? In front?

Who can cross the free foot in front of the leg they are standing on?

Can you put the free foot against the supporting leg and balance like a stork?

Can you change legs and stand on the opposite one?

Can you do all of these things with your hands on your hips?

Who can hold the *one-foot balance* for six counts with eyes closed?

Falling and Landing

Unexpected falls do not allow one to choose what kind of roll to do. Therefore, a variety of rolling techniques should be learned to the point of their becoming conditioned responses. A *conditioned response* is a sequence of muscular contractions that are preplanned and practiced to the point that they can be carried out without conscious supervision.

4. ☐ Introduced and understood
   ☐ Performs basic skill
   ☐ Conditioned response with variations

5. ☐ Introduced and understood
   ☐ Performs basic skill
   ☐ Conditioned response with variations

6. ☐ Introduced and understood
   ☐ Performs basic skill
   ☐ Conditioned response with variations

4. Dog Roll

DESCRIPTION:

Begin on hands and knees. Lower hip to one side, then lower that same shoulder so that body rolls across back with hips and shoulders touching mat. Then continue over to *hands-and-knees position* by raising shoulders and then hips.

VARIATIONS:

Can you roll across your back very smoothly?
Who can roll back in the opposite direction?
Can you lower your shoulder first as you begin your *dog roll?*
Who can begin on all fours with knees off the mat?
Can you also finish on all fours with knees off the mat?
Can you do the *dog roll* slowly with your eyes closed?

5. Sit Back from Squat

DESCRIPTION:

From a standing position squat down until seat is against heels, hands are on mat in front of body, and knees are off mat between elbows. This is the *squat position*. Now keep head held forward with chin close to chest as you sit back, take weight onto buttocks, and then continue rolling down back and up onto shoulders. Then rock forward to sitting position.

VARIATIONS:

Can you let yourself back slowly and smoothly?

Can you hold a scarf or handkerchief between your chin and chest all the way through from the beginning?

Who can straighten their legs when they rock back?

Who can straighten just one leg? And the other leg?

Who can start from the *look behind position* with seat raised, then sit down onto heels and sit back all in one continuous flow?

6. Sit Back to Dog Roll

DESCRIPTION:

Begin in *squat position*. Sit back on buttocks and continue rocking back to shoulders. Balance there for a moment, then bring legs down to one side with knees tucked under, and roll sideways to hands and knees.

VARIATIONS:

Who can roll easily and smoothly?

Can you make the roll with your eyes closed?

Can you roll to the opposite side?

Can you make a ¼ turn on the way back, then side roll out?

Can you make a ¼ turn in the opposite direction?

Inverted Agility

Reaching down to take the body weight onto the arms can be a challenging experience. After successfully completing the novice inverted agility movements most performers will be strong in the arms and shoulders and aware of the legs raising up behind and overhead. Nonetheless, a performer carrying extra weight or a bit weak in the arms can learn these movements more easily by placing the hands onto a mat pile or some stable surface (tumbling table) that is raised off the floor. In this way the performer does not fall to the floor and there is a more gentle transfer of weight from feet to hands and back to feet. The raised surface helps a performer return the foot under the center of gravity, thus making it possible to come back to the standing position.

4.
☐ Introduced and understood
☐ Performs basic skill
☐ Conditioned response with variations

5.
☐ Introduced and understood
☐ Performs basic skill
☐ Conditioned response with variations

6.
☐ Introduced and understood
☐ Performs basic skill
☐ Conditioned response with variations

4. Kick Up

DESCRIPTION:
Stand with one foot in front of the other. Now reach down, bending at hips, and put hands on mat as back leg is kicked up behind. Kick high enough that supporting foot is momentarily lifted off mat.

VARIATIONS:
Can you come back to the starting position, standing on your feet?

Can you kick just barely hard enough to raise the supporting foot off the mat? *Do you put the supporting foot back in the same place on the mat? You should!* Keep working on this until you can.

Can you kick your leg a little higher? **Caution:** Do not kick so high that you fall over your head. Can you hesitate for just a moment standing on your hands with legs in the air?

Who can momentarily touch the feet together at the top of the kick?

5. Switch-a-Roo

DESCRIPTION:

Begin standing, one foot forward, leaning down prepared to kick rear leg upward. Lean onto arms, kick rear leg up behind so that trailing foot comes off floor. Then quickly bring high leg down to floor for support as the other leg switches places with it.

VARIATIONS:

Can you bend your knees as they kick upward?

Can you straighten your legs as they kick upward?

Can you lead with the opposite leg?

How high can you kick the leading leg? **Caution:** Do not kick so high that you fall over your head.

Can you start on one side of a straight line, straddle it with your hands, and finish on the other side of that line?

6. Barrel Roll

DESCRIPTION:

Stand facing a line on floor that runs horizontally across in front. As you lean forward, your hands and shoulders make a ¼ twist toward leading foot. Then execute *switch-a-roo* with hands straddling line, ending on other side of line.

VARIATIONS:

Can you go back across the line leading with the opposite leg?

Can you finish facing the place where you started?

Do you bend your knees as you kick upward? Can you make them straight?

Can you straddle your legs wide as you kick?

As you land can you balance on the landing foot?

Inverted Balance

Note: These movements should *not* be required of any child who expresses discomfort or fear.

    Caution: If the novice activities for inverted balance have been mastered, the neck will be sufficiently strong to accomplish all these movements. The novice activities must be mastered prior to attempting these activities.

    Inverted balance is an excellent activity for the development of orientation in space and inner ear stimulation.

4.
- ☐ Introduced and understood
- ☐ Performs basic skill
- ☐ Conditioned response with variations

5.
- ☐ Introduced and understood
- ☐ Performs basic skill
- ☐ Conditioned response with variations

6.
- ☐ Introduced and understood
- ☐ Performs basic skill
- ☐ Conditioned response with variations

4. One Free Knee

DESCRIPTION:

    Come to *tripod position.* Then raise one knee off elbow.

VARIATIONS:

    After your knee is off the elbow, can you move it from side to side?

    Can you wiggle your foot?

    Can you cross your legs at the ankles?

    Can you change which knee is free?

    Who can clap their feet together?

    Who can close their eyes and still hold their balance for six counts?

5. One Straight Leg

DESCRIPTION:

Come to *tripod position*. Then raise one knee off elbow and allow that leg to straighten out.

VARIATIONS:

Can you wiggle your foot?

Can you tap the floor with the toes on your free foot?

Can you change legs so that the opposite leg is free?

Who can point at the wall with their free toes? What else can you point at?

Can you bend and straighten the free leg?

Can you hold your balance for six counts with your eyes closed?

6. Double Free Knee

DESCRIPTION:

Come to *tripod position*. Then hold hips upward so that both knees can come off elbows.

VARIATIONS:

Can you hold this balance for six counts?

Can you hold your balance perfectly still?

Can you clap your knees together?

Can you clap your feet together?

Who can cross their feet at the ankles?

Can you hold this balance for six counts with your eyes closed?

Upright Agility

With matured strength in the legs and better balance and control of the body in general, children can now begin to leap higher and perform a wider range of activities while suspended. The agile movements should in general be executed on the way upward so that coming down can be used to prepare for landing.

Caution: It is very important to land with knees slightly bent, back rounded, and shoulders leaning forward. (Landing with shoulders behind hips can easily cause a back injury.)

4.
☐ Introduced and understood
☐ Performs basic skill
☐ Conditioned response with variations

5.
☐ Introduced and understood
☐ Performs basic skill
☐ Conditioned response with variations

6.
☐ Introduced and understood
☐ Performs basic skill
☐ Conditioned response with variations

4. Seat Kicker

DESCRIPTION:
Leap into air with both arms stretched upward; quickly flex knees so that heels come up and kick buttocks. Then quickly bring feet down to land in *balanced landing position.*

VARIATIONS:
Can you kick your seat with your knees together? Knees apart?
Can you swing your arms upward vigorously above your head?
Can you kick your seat and land facing to the side?
Can you kick your seat and land facing backward?

IMAGERY:
A drop of water happened to fall into a hot skillet. That drop of water just kept hopping and hopping in the air until it finally hopped right out of the skillet.

5. Straddle Jump

DESCRIPTION:
Leap upward and lift toes outward and forward of body; then quickly bring feet back under body to land *on balance* with shoulders forward in safe landing position.

CAUTION:
Emphasize landing with shoulders forward and knees slightly bent!

VARIATIONS:
Can you hold your balance when you land?

How high can you leap?

How wide can you get your feet and still get them back under you for landing?

Who can make a ¼ twist as they leap upward and land facing to one side?

6. Stride Leap

DESCRIPTION:
Stand with one foot forward. Swing trailing foot upward in front of body and leap forward to land on that foot.

VARIATIONS:
Can you hold your balance on one foot when you land?

Who can kick their foot higher? Can you still land on balance?

Can you change feet to kick the opposite foot in the air?

Can you swing your arms upward for lift? Can you hold your arms outward like wings?

Can you land on a predetermined spot on the mat?

Can you leap over a predetermined distance?

How far can you leap and still keep control?

Rolling Over Forward

Complete rotation of the body requires good integration of the sensory and muscle systems. Successful completion of the 360-degree rotation is a great confidence builder. All will be pleased and proud of their accomplishment.

Turning over the head creates an orientation problem. First the head tucks under the body, thus giving up the visual point of reference, and then the feet leave the mat and are no longer the source of support, thus giving up the kinesthetic point of reference. Yet, by repeating the *tip over* the interval of disorientation gradually gets shorter and shorter until finally the performer can actually be thinking about what he or she wants to do upon recovery. When the performers can reorient quickly they are ready to complete the turn and return to a standing position. The *seat lifter* is therefore a very important part of getting off the floor smoothly.

4.
- ☐ Introduced and understood
- ☐ Performs basic skill
- ☐ Conditioned response with variations

5.
- ☐ Introduced and understood
- ☐ Performs basic skill
- ☐ Conditioned response with variations

6.
- ☐ Introduced and understood
- ☐ Performs basic skill
- ☐ Conditioned response with variations

4. Tip Over

DESCRIPTION:

Begin in *squat position*. Then straighten legs and tuck chin under to look for ceiling as back of head is placed on mat. Hips continue rising until they "tip over" head. Finish in sitting position.

VARIATIONS:

Who can see the ceiling as they tip over?
Can you sit up straight after you tip over?
Can you grab your knees as you raise to the sitting position?

IMAGERY:

You are hopping along like a bunny. You hear something behind you so you stop and look back between your legs, but you look back so fast that your seat tips over your head. You quickly get back to your hands and feet and hop back to your hole in the ground.

5. Seat Lifter

DESCRIPTION:

From sitting, rock backward, then rock forward pulling heels in close to seat. Reach out over feet with head and hands so far that seat comes off mat.

VARIATIONS:

When you rock forward, can you touch your chest to your legs?

When you rock forward, can you cross your legs at the ankles? (This will help those who cannot get their seat off the floor when their knees are in front of them.)

INSTRUCTOR'S ASSISTANCE:

Ask the students to sit on mat. You approach them from the front with both of your hands outstretched, palms upward, and say, "Give me ten." The students reach forward and slap your hands. Back away an inch or two and repeat. Each time the student must reach out farther to hit your hands. Finally ask the students to do a *back rocker* and as they come forward reach out and "give you ten."

6. Forward Roll

DESCRIPTION:

Begin standing. Then squat down, tip over forward, and continue rolling up onto feet and back to standing.

VARIATIONS:

Can you reach your hands out forward as you are raising your seat?

Can you grab your knees as you are raising your seat?

Who can roll easily and smoothly?

Who can roll faster? Who can roll very slowly?

Who can hop on both feet before they squat and do the *forward roll?*

Who can hop on both feet after they do the *forward roll?*

Rolling Over Backward

Even at the intermediate level the student still does not roll backward directly over the head. More preparation is required. These activities bring the roll from across the middle of the back up to the shoulder. Beginning with the *arm roll* the knee goes out over the arm. The *back rocker* prior to the *arm roll* puts the point of roll closer to the shoulder. These rolls are very good protective activities for falling and landing.

4. ☐ Introduced and understood
☐ Performs basic skill
☐ Conditioned response with variations

5. ☐ Introduced and understood
☐ Performs basic skill
☐ Conditioned response with variations

6. ☐ Introduced and understood
☐ Performs basic skill
☐ Conditioned response with variations

4. Arm Roll

DESCRIPTION:

Begin in *back balance*, arms downward by the side and pressed against mat, legs bent with knees pulled in toward forehead. Allow legs to fall to one side, rolling over arm. Bring body to *hands-and-knees position*.

VARIATIONS:

Can you roll smoothly over the arm and up to your hands and knees?

Can you fall to the opposite side? Which side seems easier for you?

Can you do the roll with your eyes closed? Feel your body all the way through. Where is the most awkward spot for you?

5. Back Rocker to Arm Roll

6. Back Shoulder Roll

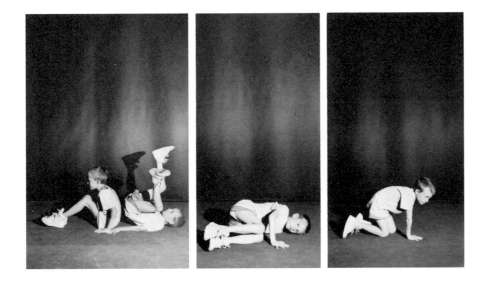

DESCRIPTION:

From sitting on mat, rock back through the *back balance position* (with arms at sides against mat) and immediately fall over one arm to an *arm roll*.

VARIATIONS:

Can you roll over the arm smoothly?

Are your legs bent? They should be.

Can you look to one side before you begin the *back rocker* and do a ¼ turn as you rock back? Does this make the *arm roll* easier?

DESCRIPTION:

Begin sitting on mat with hands on mat in front of hips. Partially turn shoulders to one side. Look to that side with head. Now rock back and extend legs up over shoulder and continue on over to mat beyond. As you press shoulder against mat one leg may extend out straight, the other knee should come quickly down to catch your weight. The shoulder you roll over stays down; the other hand comes over your head to press against mat. Recover to hands and knees.

COMMENTS:

This move is very difficult to describe and often difficult to understand from the performer's point of view. Yet when falling backward it is very advantageous to be able to move the head to one side and roll over the shoulder. Those who learn this movement have a very useful safety maneuver.

Intermediate Springboard Activities

Forward Bouncing

At the intermediate level the children will be familiar with the springboard and therefore more apt to bounce higher and farther than novices do. You will also note that there is a tendency for children to back up and run at the springboard.

Teacher's Note: You can limit running space by placing the springboard about 8 feet from the wall and turning it so that the approach is from that direction. It is also important to emphasize again the *landing position* with knees and waist slightly bent and shoulders leaning forward.

4.
- ☐ Introduced and understood
- ☐ Performs basic skill
- ☐ Conditioned response with variations

5.
- ☐ Introduced and understood
- ☐ Performs basic skill
- ☐ Conditioned response with variations

6.
- ☐ Introduced and understood
- ☐ Performs basic skill
- ☐ Conditioned response with variations

4. Tuck Bounce

DESCRIPTION:

Bounce off end of board, quickly pull knees up toward chest, then quickly reach down with legs to recover in *landing position*.

VARIATIONS:

Can you grab your knees with your hands when you pull your legs up?

Can you pull your knees up tightly?

Can you hold your arms out like wings?

Can you reach your arms upward overhead?

Can you land and balance on a target?

5. Straddle Bounce

DESCRIPTION:

Bounce off end of board; quickly straddle legs outward and upward to bend slightly at hips. Then quickly bring legs back under body to recover in *landing position.*

VARIATIONS:

Can you land on a target?

Can you balance when you land? Can you hold your landing for three counts?

Can you straddle a little wider?

Can you keep your legs straight?

Can you point your toes as an extension of your legs?

Can you extend your arms out parallel to your legs?

6. Stretch Bounce

DESCRIPTION:

Bounce off end of board, reach upward with arms and pull knees and legs backward behind hips in a stretched position, then quickly bend hips and recover to *landing position.*

VARIATIONS:

Can you swing your arms upward to get more height?

Can you land on your target?

Can you hold your landing for three counts?

Who can bend their knees so that the heels come up toward a *seat kicker?*

Twisting

Caution: These activities should *not* be done from a run. Children should take no more than one or two steps and bounce upward not outward. The reason for this is that lateral motion could cause injury to the knees.

Children will love turning in the air and landing facing different directions. Review twisting on the mats as a warm up.

4. ¼ Twist

DESCRIPTION:

Take one or two steps and bounce upward off springboard. Before landing twist hips and feet to one side (*¼ twist*). Finish in *landing position.*

VARIATIONS:

Can you land *on balance?*
Can you twist your head and shoulders on the way up?
Can you twist in the opposite direction?

4. ☐ Introduced and understood
☐ Performs basic skill
☐ Conditioned response with variations

5. ☐ Introduced and understood
☐ Performs basic skill
☐ Conditioned response with variations

6. ☐ Introduced and understood
☐ Performs basic skill
☐ Conditioned response with variations

5. ½ Twist

6. ¾ Twist

DESCRIPTION:

Take one step and bounce upward and off springboard. As you are rising turn head and shoulders to face backward; then allow body to follow. Bring hips in alignment as you recover to *landing position.*

VARIATIONS:

Can you raise your arms overhead on the upward bounce?

Can you see the person behind you as you land?

Can you say "Hello" and call his or her name?

Can you twist in the opposite direction?

Do you prefer twisting in one direction rather than the other?

TEACHER'S NOTE:

A number of factors could affect this preference, including dominant eye, dominant hand, dominant foot, dominant ear, and inner ear. A combination of these factors will influence this preference.

DESCRIPTION:

Take one step and bounce up and off springboard. Before landing make *¾ twist.* Finish in *landing position.*

TEACHER'S NOTE:

Designate a specific wall or spot to face upon landing. Allow children who prefer twisting the opposite direction to face the other wall.

VARIATIONS:

Can you raise your arms overhead on the upward bounce?

Can you land *on balance?* Can you hold the balance for three counts?

Can you see a spot on the wall before you land?

Rolling Sequence

Caution: At the intermediate level, serial memory becomes very important. Quite often a child will notice that the activity begins with a bounce off the springboard and ends with a roll over the head, but will absolutely forget that there was a landing in between. If the teacher does not take preventative action, he or she will be shocked to see a child literally dive off the springboard. You can prevent this from happening: be sure to have the children count, "one, two," while they are balanced on their feet between the landing and the roll.

These sequences of bouncing, landing, and rolling are among the most fun and rewarding activities in gymnastics. The children feel a great deal of accomplishment and the kinesthetic systems are stimulated to a higher level of sensitivity and response.

4.
☐ Introduced and understood
☐ Performs basic skill
☐ Conditioned response with variations

5.
☐ Introduced and understood
☐ Performs basic skill
☐ Conditioned response with variations

6.
☐ Introduced and understood
☐ Performs basic skill
☐ Conditioned response with variations

4. Knee Slapper—Tip Over

CAUTION:

Children tend to forget to land on their feet. They could dive headfirst, which is very dangerous. Be sure to have the children practice landing on their feet and count, "one, two," before continuing to *tip over.*

DESCRIPTION:

Bounce off springboard and execute *knee slapper.* After landing on feet, count, "one, two," then bend knees to slight *squat*, place hands on floor, and execute *tip over.*

VARIATIONS:

Can you do a *lame dog walk* before the *tip over?*
Can you do a *bunny hop* before the *tip over?*
Can you land on a target?

5. Seat Kicker—Tip Over

CAUTION:

Be sure to have the children practice landing on their feet before continuing to the *tip over*. Otherwise they might dive headfirst, which is very dangerous.

DESCRIPTION:

Bounce off springboard and execute *seat kicker*. After landing on feet, bend knees to slight *squat*, place hands on floor, and execute *tip over*.

VARIATIONS:

Can you do the *lame dog walk* before the *tip over?*
Can you do the *bunny hop* before the *tip over?*
Can you swing your arms upward on the *seat kicker?*

6. Seat Kicker—Forward Roll

CAUTION:

Again, be sure to have the children practice landing on their feet before rolling.

DESCRIPTION:

Bounce off springboard and execute *seat kicker*. After landing on feet, bend knees to slight *squat*, place hands on floor, and execute *forward roll*.

VARIATIONS:

Can you swing your arms upward during the *seat kicker?*
Can you finish the *forward roll* with one foot in front of the other?
Can you finish the roll with ¼ turn upon standing?
Can you cross your legs at the ankles upon finishing the *forward roll* and turn to face backward?

With Table

To rebound means that the legs are tense and they literally hit the table in a pushing-away action instead of landing and then as a separate motion jumping up and off. This rebounding action can be practiced on the floor with a sequence of four or five continuous bounces.

This activity stimulates the reflex system and allows the response system to develop anticipatory action while still airborne.

4.
☐ Introduced and understood
☐ Performs basic skill
☐ Conditioned response with variations

5.
☐ Introduced and understood
☐ Performs basic skill
☐ Conditioned response with variations

6.
☐ Introduced and understood
☐ Performs basic skill
☐ Conditioned response with variations

4. Rebound

DESCRIPTION:

Springboard is about 10 inches from end of tumbling table (stable and firm surface about 16 inches high). Bounce off springboard; as feet approach table, immediately push off (rebound) table and land on mats. Finish in *landing position.*

VARIATIONS:

Can you bounce twice on the table?
Can you bounce just once on the table?
Can you make a ¼ turn before landing?

5. Rebound—Knee Slapper

DESCRIPTION:

Springboard is placed about 10 inches from tumbling table. Bounce off springboard, rebound off table, and execute *knee slapper* before landing on mat. Finish in *landing position.*

VARIATIONS:

Can you slap your knees twice?

Can you make a ¼ turn before landing?

Can you execute a *knee slapper* between the springboard and the table?

Can you do one *knee slapper* between the springboard and table, and another *knee slapper* between the table and the mat?

6. Rebound—Seat Kicker

DESCRIPTION:

Springboard is about 10 inches from tumbling table. Bounce off springboard, rebound off table, and execute a *seat kicker* before landing on mat. Finish in *landing position.*

VARIATIONS:

Can you lift your arms upward during your *seat kicker?*

Can you make a ¼ turn before landing?

Can you execute the *seat kicker* between the springboard and the tumbling table?

Can you do one *seat kicker* between the springboard and the table and another between the tumbling table and the mat?

Intermediate Low Horizontal Bar Activities

Swinging Under

At the intermediate level children gain more grip strength and arm strength and more confidence in their arms as a source of support.

Review: It is important to review the novice activities to warm up the body and to update the conditioned responses to the patterns of muscle contraction that produce these swinging under activities.

4.
- ☐ Introduced and understood
- ☐ Performs basic skill
- ☐ Conditioned response with variations

5.
- ☐ Introduced and understood
- ☐ Performs basic skill
- ☐ Conditioned response with variations

6.
- ☐ Introduced and understood
- ☐ Performs basic skill
- ☐ Conditioned response with variations

4. Run Under

DESCRIPTION:

Stand facing bar, take *double over grip*. Begin walking feet under bar as shoulders lean backward and arms stay straight. After walking under bar all the way to a stretched hang, walk backward to standing.

VARIATIONS:

Can you lean back so that you walk under smoothly?
Can you go a little faster?
Can you do two in a row?
Can you do a ½ turn on the forward swing so that you end up standing facing the opposite direction?

5. Run Under and Arch

DESCRIPTION:

Stand facing bar, take *double over grip,* and execute *run under.* At farthest point of underswing, push hips upward so that body is arched. Then walk backward back to hanging under bar.

VARIATIONS:

Can you lift your chest as you arch so that your ears are between your arms?

Can you return by backing up to a stand?

Can you do two in a row?

Can you arch so vigorously that you let go of the bar and come up to a standing position? (Teacher should stand by the bar to ensure that the student does not fall back into the bar.)

6. Squat—Kick over Line

DESCRIPTION:

Stand facing bar with toes in line with bar supports. Take *double over grip,* then lean back and squat to nearly sitting on heels with arms straight. Kick one foot up in front as if taking a giant step, bring other foot up with first, and swing out over line on mat about 2 feet beyond bar. Feet touch mat just beyond line, knees push toward toes, and hips rise to an arch. Then return to hanging under bar.

VARIATIONS:

Can you bring your feet closer to the bar as you swing under?

Can you hold your legs up long enough to carry them over the line?

Can you arch so vigorously that you are pulled away from the bar to a standing position?

Support above Bar

Support above the bar now progresses to lifting the knees and legs. This additional height will cause the shoulders to lean to one side and put a little more weight on one arm than the other. This shifting of weight provides much kinesthetic input and increases the level of body awareness.

4.
☐ Introduced and understood
☐ Performs basic skill
☐ Conditioned response with variations

5.
☐ Introduced and understood
☐ Performs basic skill
☐ Conditioned response with variations

6.
☐ Introduced and understood
☐ Performs basic skill
☐ Conditioned response with variations

4. Knee Touch

DESCRIPTION:
While in *front support*, lift one knee up to touch bar beyond hand. Then repeat using other knee.

VARIATIONS:
Do you keep your arms straight?
Do you touch your knee to the top side of the bar?
Do you lean toward the arm away from the lifted knee?
Who can lift their knee even higher than the bar?

5. Toe Touch

DESCRIPTION:

From *front support,* raise one foot and touch toes to bar. Repeat using other foot.

VARIATIONS:

Does the tip of your toe touch the bar?

Can you put your foot on top of the bar?

Who can step on top of the bar with the knee lifted and bent?

Can you do it with the other foot?

6. One Leg Over

DESCRIPTION:

From *front support,* raise one leg over bar and sit for a moment on that leg. Then return leg to *front support* position.

VARIATIONS:

Can you put your weight on the leg and use your hands for balance?

Can you put the opposite leg over?

Who can balance so well that they can raise one hand off the bar for a moment?

Who can hold their balance for five seconds?

Can you bring your leg back over the bar without hitting your foot?

Grip Changes and Turning

Changing the grip affects the feelings of support and thus the confidence of the performer. By using these different types of support with movements that are already familiar, the child can gain the necessary confidence.

4. ☐ Introduced and understood
☐ Performs basic skill
☐ Conditioned response with variations

5. ☐ Introduced and understood
☐ Performs basic skill
☐ Conditioned response with variations

6. ☐ Introduced and understood
☐ Performs basic skill
☐ Conditioned response with variations

4. Mixed Grip Space Walk

DESCRIPTION:
Stand facing bar and take hold of bar with palm of one hand up and palm of other hand down and thumbs around bar (this is called the *mixed grip*). Jump up to a *front support* and execute *space walk*.

VARIATIONS:
Can you balance in the *front support* as well with a *mixed grip?*
Can you change your hands so that each hand is facing opposite?
Who can do a knee touch? Does the knee touch feel better when it is toward the hand with palm toward you? (One reason for the *mixed grip* is safety during the execution of certain turning movements.)

5. Reverse Grip Space Walk

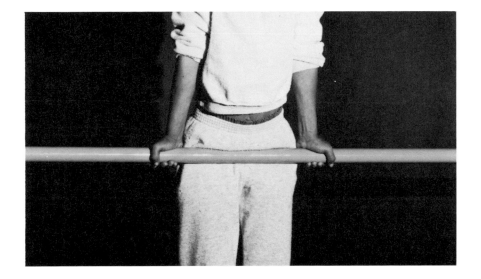

DESCRIPTION:

Stand facing bar. Take hold of bar with palms of both hands upward and thumbs around bar (this is called the *reverse grip*). Jump to *front support* with *mixed grip* and then execute *space walk*.

VARIATIONS:

Do you feel as though you will fall off backward?
Can you lean your shoulders just a little farther forward?
Some people feel safer with this grip, do you?
Can you do a *knee touch?*
Can you put one leg over the bar?

6. Front Support Slide

DESCRIPTION:

From *front support position* with *double over grip* lean sideways toward one arm, then quickly slide opposite hand close to supporting hand. When body weight shifts back again, slide free hand out to take a "step." Continue sliding one hand close and other reaching out so as to slide across bar.

VARIATIONS:

Can you wait for the shoulders to lean before you take the steps?
Can you take short fast slides?
Who can take longer slides?
Who can swing their feet as they slide?

Around the Bar

This sequence of activities will increase arm strength and abdominal strength. The integration of this additional strength along with muscular patterns and timing will be necessary to accomplish such skills as the *back pull over* in the advanced-level program.

4. ☐ Introduced and understood
   ☐ Performs basic skill
   ☐ Conditioned response with variations

5. ☐ Introduced and understood
   ☐ Performs basic skill
   ☐ Conditioned response with variations

6. ☐ Introduced and understood
   ☐ Performs basic skill
   ☐ Conditioned response with variations

4. Flexed Arm Hang

DESCRIPTION:
   Pull chest close to bar with chin over. Hold elbows in tight to ribs and lift knees up to take feet off mat.

VARIATIONS:
   Can you hold it for four seconds? Eight seconds?
   Can you clap your knees together while hanging?
   Who can hold one leg out straight?
   Can anyone hold both legs out straight?

5. Hanging Ball

DESCRIPTION:

Hold bar about even with your head as you lift knees up and close to abdomen. Legs are pulled into a *tuck posture.* Hold momentarily without allowing arms to straighten.

VARIATIONS:

Can you hold this two seconds? How about four seconds? How about eight seconds?

Can you touch your knees to the bar?

Can anyone straighten one leg and hold for two seconds?

Can anyone straighten one leg then return to the tucked position?

Can anyone alternate straightening the legs? How many counts can you make?

6. Front Roll

DESCRIPTION:

Jump to *front support,* lean forward into *bar hang,* bend knees, and continue circling over bar so that legs come over bar and lower slowly through *hanging ball position* down to mat.

VARIATIONS:

Can you let down so slowly that only one foot can catch your weight?

Can you let down so slowly that you stop in a *hanging ball?*

Can you jump up through the *front support* and roll forward immediately?

Rotating under the Bar

At the intermediate level children combine grip strength with flexibility in order to put their legs through the hands and turn over. This inverted posture helps to stimulate the inner ear and improve orientation in space.

4. ☐ Introduced and understood
   ☐ Performs basic skill
   ☐ Conditioned response with variations

5. ☐ Introduced and understood
   ☐ Performs basic skill
   ☐ Conditioned response with variations

6. ☐ Introduced and understood
   ☐ Performs basic skill
   ☐ Conditioned response with variations

4. Toe Hook

DESCRIPTION:
   While hanging under bar bring one foot up to bar and hook toe under bar.

VARIATIONS:
   Can you hook the opposite foot?
   While one toe is hooked can you bring the opposite knee up to your chest?
   Can you lift the opposite knee up between your arms?

5. Skin the Cat

DESCRIPTION:

Hang under bar. Bring first one leg and then other between arms so that body goes all the way over head and feet come down on other side.

VARIATIONS:

Arc your hands wide enough apart to get your body through the arms?

After turning over can you walk forward to stand in front of the bar?

After turning over can you reverse your direction and bring your body back through your arms?

6. The Basket

DESCRIPTION:

Hang below bar. Bring legs through arms as for *skin the cat*. Then straighten legs and lift head to face knees.

VARIATIONS:

Can you hold your legs straight and point toes outward?

Can you hold motionless for five counts?

Who can touch their thighs to their chest?

Who can push legs upward to touch the bar but not fall backward or lose balance?

Hip Casting

Hip casting at the intermediate level takes the body higher above the bar and requires more kinesthetic awareness on the dismounts. This is the first use of the term *dismount*, which refers to leaving the apparatus and landing in a controlled and balanced position.

4. ☐ Introduced and understood
   ☐ Performs basic skill
   ☐ Conditioned response with variations

5. ☐ Introduced and understood
   ☐ Performs basic skill
   ☐ Conditioned response with variations

6. ☐ Introduced and understood
   ☐ Performs basic skill
   ☐ Conditioned response with variations

4. Seat Kicker

DESCRIPTION:

In *front support* allow legs to swing forward, backward, then forward again. On second backward swing bend knees and pull heels toward buttocks to a *seat kicker*.

VARIATIONS:

If you lean forward as your legs go backward does it hold you in the air longer?

Can you keep your arms straight and your shoulders above the bar?

Can you land *on balance?*

5. ¼ Turn Dismount

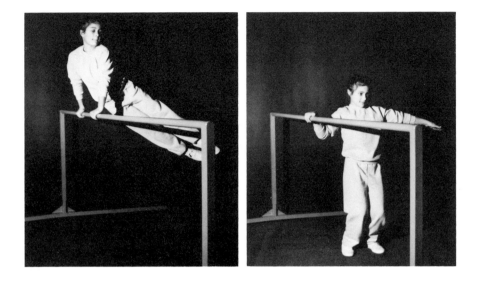

DESCRIPTION:

Swing to *seat kicker;* as feet come down push away from bar and turn to right (or left) to recover in *balanced landing position.*

VARIATIONS:

Can you get balanced without taking even a tiny step?

Can you go high on the *seat kicker* before doing ¼ *turn?*

6. ½ Turn Dismount

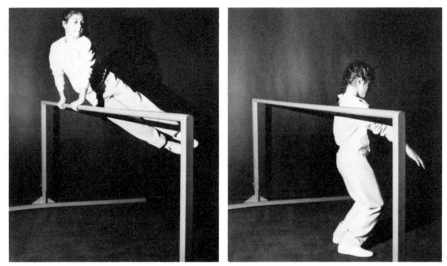

DESCRIPTION:

Swing to *seat kicker;* as feet start downward push off and turn around to *balanced landing* facing opposite direction.

VARIATIONS:

Can you start your hips turning before you let go of the bar?

Can you get your balance without taking extra steps after landing?

Does it feel uncomfortable to turn in the opposite direction?

Intermediate Tumbling Table Activities

Vaulting Over

Vaulting develops leg strength and, because of the flight and landing, requires timing and agility. Children especially enjoy this activity and like to run into a vault. Ensure that each step is taken in order and mastered before moving on to the more difficult ones.

4. ☐ Introduced and understood
☐ Performs basic skill
☐ Conditioned response with variations

5. ☐ Introduced and understood
☐ Performs basic skill
☐ Conditioned response with variations

6. ☐ Introduced and understood
☐ Performs basic skill
☐ Conditioned response with variations

4. Switch-a-Roo

DESCRIPTION:
   Place hands on level table and kick one leg upward; then quickly switch legs.

VARIATIONS:
   How high can you kick?
   Can you keep your arms straight?
   Can you finish with one leg still held high?
   Can you push your hips up high over your head and shoulders?
   Do you lean your shoulders out over your hands?
   Can you kick the opposite leg first?

5. Straddle Switch

6. Barrel Roll

DESCRIPTION:

Stand in *straddle position* facing corner of table. Bend forward at hips, place hands on table, and execute *straddle switch* by alternately raising one leg and then the other upward and out to the side.

VARIATIONS:

Who can keep their legs straight?

How wide are your legs straddled?

Can you keep the legs straddled while you switch?

How high can you raise your feet? As high as the table? As high as your head?

DESCRIPTION:

Step up to level table and prepare to kick as for a *switch-a-roo*. Hands are placed toward center of table, one hand forward of the other, with fingers facing to one side. Leg goes all the way over table and catches weight on the opposite side.

VARIATIONS:

Can you reach your leg over the table without hitting it?

Can you kick hard enough to go all the way over?

Can you keep your legs straight?

Can you straddle wide as you kick over?

Can you finish facing back where you started?

Are your fingers facing to the side? Does your leading hand reach out over the trailing hand? Shoulder too?

TEACHER'S NOTE:

Reaching out with the leading arm and shoulder to turn to one side will make the movement smoother.

Rolling Forward

In the early stages of rolling it is safer to roll up the incline than down the incline. This is not the natural approach that any of us would take and children, if left on their own, will attempt to roll down the hill. However, going upward requires less rotation of the head and the hips do not have as far to fall since the incline comes up to meet them. In addition, coming off the high end makes standing up very easy and also makes it possible to rise in a *straddle* or step out in other ways with the feet.

4.
- ☐ Introduced and understood
- ☐ Performs basic skill
- ☐ Conditioned response with variations

5.
- ☐ Introduced and understood
- ☐ Performs basic skill
- ☐ Conditioned response with variations

6.
- ☐ Introduced and understood
- ☐ Performs basic skill
- ☐ Conditioned response with variations

4. Kick Roll Up

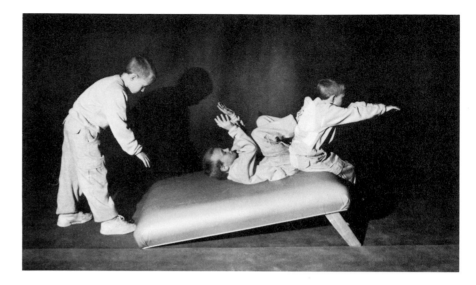

DESCRIPTION:

Stand at lower end of slanted table. Place hands on table and look back between legs as back of head touches table. Kick one leg up and over so body rolls up table.

CAUTION:

If the hands are too far up the table, there is too little room to finish sitting comfortably on the table.

VARIATIONS:

Do you come back to your feet?

Can you leap as you finish the roll?

Can you leap up with a ¼ turn? How about a ½ turn? How about a full turn?

Can you lean down after the roll on the table and do another roll on the mat?

5. Roll Up—Straddle

DESCRIPTION:

While rolling up slanted table, straddle legs; then lean forward off table to a *straddle stand* on mat.

VARIATIONS:

Can you keep your legs straight?

Can you straddle wide?

Can you finish with your arms stretched wide?

From the *straddle stand* can you lean down and do a *forward roll?*

6. Step, Jump, Roll Up

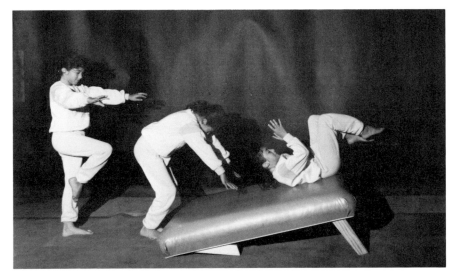

DESCRIPTION:

Stand about 5 feet back from low end of slanted table. Take one step, bounce off both feet, and roll up table.

CAUTION:

It is very important to place hands and head near the low end; otherwise, there is not enough room to roll.

VARIATIONS:

When you finish the roll can you leap in the air?

Can you do a ¼ turn? A ½ turn? How about a full turn?

Can you follow the roll up the table with a roll on the mat?

Can you come off the table with one foot in front of the other?

Rolling Backward

The slanted table gives the student the very best situation for learning to turn over backward. If the novice program has been mastered, children will have much success and pleasure rolling backward.

Caution: It is very important not to pass over step 4, Hands on Mat. This step prepares the arms and shoulders to take some of the weight off the head and neck during the roll. This step is very important for the safe and successful accomplishment of the backward rolling skills.

Teacher's Note: The *tip over* does not require that children land on their feet and thus they can be successful if they do nothing more than tip over and land on their knees. The *tip over* is placed before the *backward roll* because children need the opportunity to roll over many times without the pressure of having to think about their feet.

4.
☐ Introduced and understood
☐ Performs basic skill
☐ Conditioned response with variations

5.
☐ Introduced and understood
☐ Performs basic skill
☐ Conditioned response with variations

6.
☐ Introduced and understood
☐ Performs basic skill
☐ Conditioned response with variations

4. Hands on Mat

DESCRIPTION:

Sit on low end of slanted table with back to high end. Hold palms of hands facing away from body with thumbs pointing toward each other. Keep this relative position of hands as you raise elbows up past your ears. Palms of hands are now facing behind you, thumbs still pointing toward each other. Execute a *back rocker* and place palms of hands against mat.

VARIATIONS:

Can you feel the mat with your hands even though you cannot see it?

Can you put the palms of your hands flat against the mat?

Can you push against the mat with your hands?

If you have long hair does it get in the way of your hands? (If possible, pull hair back out of the way.)

Do you lift your elbows up above your ears even before you start to do the *back rocker?* That is good.

5. Tip Over Backward

DESCRIPTION:

   Sit on high end of slanted table with elbows raiscd, thumbs toward each other, and palms facing backward. Rock backward down table, pulling knees toward shoulders. Press hands against table to hold weight as body tips over head and falls on mat.

VARIATIONS:

   Can you feel the table with your hands?
   Can you push against the table to lift it away from your head?
   Can you rock back and tip over in one continuous motion?
   Do you land on your knees?
   Can you catch yourself on one knee only?
   Can you straddle your legs and catch yourself in a *straddle position?*

6. Backward Roll

DESCRIPTION:

   Sit on high end of slanted table with elbows raised, thumbs toward each other, and palms facing back. Rock backward down table, pulling knees toward shoulders. Press hands against table to hold weight as body tips over head. Bring feet to mat to catch weight so that knees do not touch.

VARIATIONS:

   Can you get your balance and come up on your feet?
   Do you land with your toes in line?
   Can you straddle your legs and finish in a *straddle stand?*
   Can you finish with one foot behind the other?
   Who can leap upward after the roll and do a ½ turn?

Intermediate Beam Activities

Balancing on the Level Beam

At the intermediate level the student begins to expand the balancing responses. Moving back and forth on the beam requires an ever-ready conditioned response to quickly contract muscles throughout the body for balance. Since the body is moving and constantly taking new positions, the response must always be just a little different, thus the neural system must develop a means of calculating responses according to the location and degree of imbalance.

Caution: These activities should be learned on a very low beam, below the level of the knee. Falling off will not be a danger if the children have previously learned the novice-level upright agility series on the mats as well as falling and landing.

4.
- ☐ Introduced and understood
- ☐ Performs basic skill
- ☐ Conditioned response with variations

5.
- ☐ Introduced and understood
- ☐ Performs basic skill
- ☐ Conditioned response with variations

6.
- ☐ Introduced and understood
- ☐ Performs basic skill
- ☐ Conditioned response with variations

4. Walk Forward

DESCRIPTION:

Stand on beam facing longways. Walk slowly forward taking small steps and feeling beam with each foot before putting weight on it. Turn to side and jump down to *balanced landing position.*

VARIATIONS:

Can you hold your arms out wide for balance?

Can you hold your hands on your hips? On top of your head?

Can you land in a balanced position and hold for three counts?

Can you take longer, slower steps?

Where do you look? Can you see the wall in front of you? Can you see the beam?

5. Slide to the Side

DESCRIPTION:

Stand on beam crossways. Step with one foot out to side; then slide other foot up to first. Continue stepping and sliding to the side. Stop; jump down to *balanced landing position.*

VARIATIONS:

Can you take several small steps without falling off?

Can you take larger steps? What part of your foot touches the beam?

Are your heels on the beam? Are your toes on the beam? What gives you the best balance?

Can you slide back in the opposite direction? Can you take shorter, faster steps?

Where do you hold your arms? Can you hold them out to the side? Can you lower them about halfway to your sides?

6. Walk and Pivot

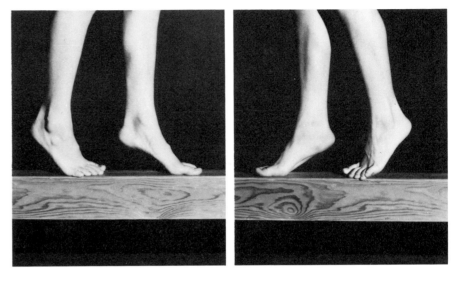

DESCRIPTION:

Stand on beam facing longways. Take one or two steps. Then lift your heels, pivot on your toes, and make a ½ turn to face opposite direction.

TEACHER'S NOTE:

Children can learn this pivot by practicing on the floor. In this way all children can do many pivots and their body will know the pattern prior to getting on the beam.

VARIATIONS:

Can you walk a few steps and pivot again? Can you take just one step and pivot again? Can you feel the beam beneath the balls of your feet?

What is the best arm position for good balance?

Can you pivot and then reverse and pivot back in the opposite direction?

Can you squat down nearly to your heels and then pivot?

Vaulting on the Level Beam

For these activities the height of the beam should be about the level of the knees of the participants.

At the intermediate level the vaulting becomes a reality. The body is carried completely over the beam with the support on the arms. This is a great sense of accomplishment for children.

The *barrel roll* is probably the smoothest way to get over a chest-high fence or obstacle. The prerequisite to a good *barrel roll* is a good *step over vault.*

The *crab vault* provides the unique situation of having the back to the beam and the arm in a rear support position.

4.
- ☐ Introduced and understood
- ☐ Performs basic skill
- ☐ Conditioned response with variations

5.
- ☐ Introduced and understood
- ☐ Performs basic skill
- ☐ Conditioned response with variations

6.
- ☐ Introduced and understood
- ☐ Performs basic skill
- ☐ Conditioned response with variations

4. Crab Vault

DESCRIPTION:

Stand straddle of beam and then sit down on beam. Raise one knee upward and place foot on beam in front. Hand on same side of body reaches behind back and is placed on beam to give support. Raise hips off beam in a *crab position.* Now swing leg still on floor up and over body. Body makes a ½ turn to land standing on floor facing opposite direction.

VARIATIONS:

Can you balance on the beam for a moment on one foot and one hand?

Can you raise the free hand high above you?

Can you kick the free leg vigorously over the beam?

Can you land in a *balanced landing position?*

Can you turn the fingers of the supporting hand to the *reverse grip position?*

5. Step Over Vault

DESCRIPTION:

Stand straddle of beam. Bend forward and place hands on beam for support. Now raise one foot backward up and over beam to touch toes behind supporting foot. From this position throw free leg back over beam as though stepping over. Trailing leg follows to finish on opposite side of beam.

VARIATIONS:

Can you alternately step from one side to the other and then back again?

Can you make a wider straddle with the legs?

Can you raise the hips higher as you step over?

6. Barrel Roll

DESCRIPTION:

Stand straddle of beam and bend forward to place hands on beam for support. Raise one foot backward up and over beam to place that foot behind supporting foot. Place all of body's weight on legs so that hands can be raised a few inches from beam. From this position lean onto arms and rapidly execute the *step over vault.* The fact that body began the motion with hands off beam makes this a *barrel roll.*

VARIATIONS:

Can you kick over and land smoothly?

As you land on the opposite side of the beam can you make a ½ turn and walk away? Can you walk up to the beam and *barrel roll* over?

Can you approach the beam from the opposite direction? Which side is easiest for you?

Can you kick your feet a little higher?

Balancing on the Slanted Beam

At this intermediate level children are jumping down from above knee height. If they have mastered upright balance on the mats at the intermediate level and forward bouncing on the springboard at the intermediate level, these activities will be well within their grasp.

These activities give children a sense of height and they integrate the visual sense with the kinesthetic feelings of resisting gravity upon landing.

4.
☐ Introduced and understood
☐ Performs basic skill
☐ Conditioned response with variations

5.
☐ Introduced and understood
☐ Performs basic skill
☐ Conditioned response with variations

6.
☐ Introduced and understood
☐ Performs basic skill
☐ Conditioned response with variations

4. Walk to Second Mark

DESCRIPTION:

Stand on slanted beam at low end facing high end. Walk slowly and carefully upward to second mark (slightly above knee height). Turn and jump down to *balanced landing position*.

VARIATIONS:

Can you walk smoothly and with rhythm?
Can you hold your hands out gracefully from the sides?
Can you put your hands on top of your head?
Can you take very small steps?
Can you take slightly larger steps?
Can you hold your balance upon landing? For three counts?

5. Slide to Second Mark

DESCRIPTION:

Stand crossways on low end of slanted beam. Step out with foot on upper side, slide other foot up to meet first. Continue step sliding to second mark (slightly above knee height). Jump down to *balanced landing position.*

VARIATIONS:

Who can take very small sliding steps?

Who can hold their arms out for balance?

Who can turn and face the opposite direction and lead with the opposite foot?

Who can invent a rhythm and style to their step slide?

6. Walk Backward to Second Mark

DESCRIPTION:

Stand on low end of slanted beam with high end to your back. Slowly and carefully walk backward up beam to second mark (slightly higher than knees). Turn and jump down to *balanced landing position.*

VARIATIONS:

Do you feel the beam with your foot before you place weight on it?

Can you move with a slow rhythm?

Where do you like to put your arms?

Can you use your hands to pretend you are pushing yourself away from the low end?

Vaulting on the Slanted Beam

To bounce up and over the beam raising both feet at the same time gives the performer a great feeling of control. The body seems light and under the control of the performer. The learner gains a great deal of self-confidence and a sense that this movement skill could provide defense against a myriad of challenges.

4.
- ☐ Introduced and understood
- ☐ Performs basic skill
- ☐ Conditioned response with variations

5.
- ☐ Introduced and understood
- ☐ Performs basic skill
- ☐ Conditioned response with variations

6.
- ☐ Introduced and understood
- ☐ Performs basic skill
- ☐ Conditioned response with variations

4. Step On Vault

DESCRIPTION:

Stand at low end of slanted beam facing high end. Bend forward and place hands on beam with palms facing each other and fingers down over side of beam (*palm-to-palm grip*). Step onto beam with inside foot. Now push with foot that is on beam in order to raise hips and other foot up and over beam to opposite side.

VARIATIONS:

Can you land in a *balanced landing position?*
Can you raise your hips a little higher?
Can you clap your feet together before you land?
Can you execute a *tuck position* before you land?
Can you turn to land facing the beam?

5. Tuck Bounce

DESCRIPTION:

Stand beside beam at low end facing high end. Place hands on beam, bounce hips up, and quickly bend knees and lift feet to *tuck position*. Quickly lower feet to recover in *balanced landing position*.

VARIATIONS:

Can you bounce a little higher?

Can you bounce two times in a row?

Do you feel the weight of your body on your arms? Can you pause just a moment at the top of your bounce?

Can you stand on the opposite side of the beam and bounce?

Can you lean your shoulders over the beam just a very slight amount?

Does this put more weight on your arms?

6. Kangaroo Hop

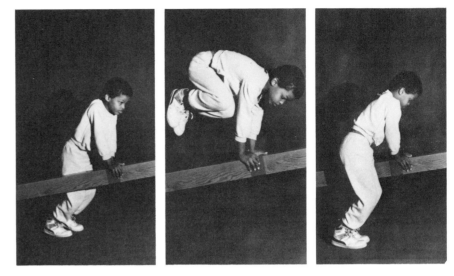

DESCRIPTION:

Stand at low end of slanted beam facing high end. Reach down and take *palm-to-palm grip*. Bounce both feet up and over beam in a *tuck position* to land on other side.

CAUTION:

You must have mastered the *tuck bounce* before attempting this skill. Be sure to lift your hips and feet up high in order to clear the beam with your feet; otherwise, your feet will catch on the beam and prevent you from a safe landing on the other side.

VARIATIONS:

Can you raise your legs high and clear the beam easily?

Can you lean over your arms and take more weight on them?

Can you bounce over, then bounce back to the side where you started?

Can you hold your feet together?

Can you take a preparatory bounce before you bounce over?

4. Advanced Program:

Students in Grades 4, 5, and 6 Who Have Completed the Intermediate Program

Advanced Mat Activities

Upright Balance

At the advanced level much more strength and sensitivity are required of the supporting leg, which functions as a *scale* (a single support with the body parts balanced on either side). The muscles in the leg must be trained to respond to slight changes in balance. Flexibility becomes increasingly important. The supporting leg is expected to carry out its balancing task even though the conscious mind is involved with activities in the free limbs. The free limbs of the body are taken through a greater range of motion and must be very sensitive to their task in acting as ballast.

7.
- ☐ Introduced and understood
- ☐ Performs basic skill
- ☐ Conditioned response with variations

8.
- ☐ Introduced and understood
- ☐ Performs basic skill
- ☐ Conditioned response with variations

9.
- ☐ Introduced and understood
- ☐ Performs basic skill
- ☐ Conditioned response with variations

7. Knee Lifter

DESCRIPTION:

Stand straight and erect. Hold arms out for ballast and raise one knee in front of body to balance on one foot.

VARIATIONS:

Can you hold your balance for six counts?

Can you be very still while you balance?

Can you breathe while you are balancing? Feel yourself breathing.

Can you raise the knee up as high as your waist?

Can you grasp your knee with your hand?

While holding your knee with your hand, can you pull the knee outward to the side?

Who can take hold of their ankle with their hand and hold it while they balance?

Can you do all of this while balancing on the opposite foot?

8. Bent Hip Scale

DESCRIPTION:

Stand on firm surface. (Some mats are not firm enough for good balance.) Balance on one foot, lean trunk of body forward with arms outward for ballast, and raise foot of free leg behind as high as your waist. Free knee can be bent so as to raise foot more easily.

VARIATIONS:

Can you balance very still? Can you take in a big breath and let it out?

Close your eyes momentarily and notice the muscles in your supporting leg. Can they keep you balanced even with your eyes closed? How long? Can you bend your shoulders farther forward?

Can you reach down with one hand and just barely touch the floor with your finger? Can you touch the floor with the opposite hand? When you try the opposite hand, what happens to the free leg?

9. Extended Hip Scale

DESCRIPTION:

Stand on firm surface. Stand erect, chest out, arms extended upward and outward. Carefully balance on one foot by extending opposite leg behind body so as to arch back. Knee may be bent but hip cannot be bent with reference to free leg (hip will be bent with reference to supporting leg).

VARIATIONS:

Can you raise your free leg slightly higher behind you?

How high can you raise your free leg and still hold the extended body position?

Does your supporting leg want to bend? Let it bend. Now can you make the supporting leg straight?

Can you raise your free leg (with knee bent) until your foot is as high as your head?

How can you vary the position of your arms without losing the extension of the free knee and hip?

Falling and Landing

Finally, at the advanced level, we approach falling and landing from the standing position. From standing, the value of a good roll is more obvious. We cannot emphasize too much that during an actual fall there is not enough time to plan what is to be done. Therefore, all rolls and falls should be practiced over and over again until they are carried out as a subconscious pattern. This is referred to as a *conditioned response.* When the body is falling, the subconscious will quickly call upon the most appropriate conditioned response that is programmed and ready for use. Without training, there will not be a large repertoire of responses to fit any particular situation.

7.
☐ Introduced and understood
☐ Performs basic skill
☐ Conditioned response with variations

8.
☐ Introduced and understood
☐ Performs basic skill
☐ Conditioned response with variations

9.
☐ Introduced and understood
☐ Performs basic skill
☐ Conditioned response with variations

7. Standing Sit Back

DESCRIPTION:
Stand with mat behind. Bend knees and lower toward *squat position,* then sit back onto mat so as to smoothly roll into a *back rocker.*

VARIATIONS:
Do you touch the mat with the palms of your hands, fingers pointing forward?

Can you lower onto the mat a bit faster?

Can you take a hop on your feet before the *sit back?*

Can you turn as you sit back so as to move your head out of the line of roll?

Can you face the mat, jump with a ½ turn, and immediately sit back?

Can you face to one side and twist your body as you lower into a *sit back?*

8. Back Shoulder Roll

DESCRIPTION:

Stand with mat behind. Squat down to *back rocker* and continue legs over shoulder to *shoulder roll.*

VARIATIONS:

How smoothly can you make the roll?

Can you take your opposite hand across your face to press against the mat?

Do you finish on your hands and knees? Can you finish standing?

Can you stand facing the mat and jump with a ½ turn before the *back shoulder roll?*

Can you take several hops backward before the roll?

9. Paratrooper's Fall

DESCRIPTION:

Stand facing mat. Hold hands and forearms up in front as though holding support straps of a parachute. Squat down as if to sit on heels and pivot on balls of feet so that both knees move to one side. Knee and leg closest to mat fall to mat as body twists over buttocks to a *back rocker.*

VARIATIONS:

Can you make the squat and twist smooth so as to ease the body to the mat?

Do you twist on your back to face to one side?

Can you use the twist to the knees as a way to enter a *back shoulder roll?* (In this case do not hold the arms upward.)

Inverted Agility

With the novice and intermediate experiences mastered, every performer will enjoy these advanced inverted agility activities, which culminate with the *cartwheel*. Every performer is proud to demonstrate these activities, which exhibit their skill and dexterity. Having the feet above the head is fun when the performer knows that the body is under control. For this reason do not rush to the *cartwheel*, but cover very thoroughly the *high kick* and the *switch-a-roo-roo* since these movements are prerequisite to the successful execution of the *cartwheel*.

7.
- ☐ Introduced and understood
- ☐ Performs basic skill
- ☐ Conditioned response with variations

8.
- ☐ Introduced and understood
- ☐ Performs basic skill
- ☐ Conditioned response with variations

9.
- ☐ Introduced and understood
- ☐ Performs basic skill
- ☐ Conditioned response with variations

7. High Kick

DESCRIPTION:

Stand, arms stretched high overhead, one foot forward of the other. With a continuous motion reach forward and down; kick upward with trailing leg so that body weight is taken completely by arms. Allow body to come back down to starting position.

VARIATIONS:

How high does the leading leg go? Is it straight above your head?

Can you keep your arms stretched and straight?

Can you come back to the starting position with your arms stretched overhead?

Can you keep the supporting leg extended as you kick up? And come down?

8. Switch-a-Roo-Roo

DESCRIPTION:

Stand beside a line. Foot away from line comes forward and in front of the other. Stretch arms overhead. Reach down as in *high kick* but with hands on either side of line. Allow leading leg to rise high overhead as weight comes equally onto arms. Then legs trade places and body comes down on opposite side of line.

VARIATIONS:

Are your legs extended high above your head?

Can you pause just a moment as your legs get ready to change jobs? Do you stand right by the line? Can you stand a few inches away and finish the same distance away on the other side?

9. Cartwheel

DESCRIPTION:

Stand facing a line, one foot forward. Stretch hands above head so that arm and shoulder on same side of forward foot are also slightly forward. Reach downward, bending at hips, and kick trailing leg up. As leg rises, hands are placed straddling line and accept body weight. Leading leg continues over body and comes down on opposite side of line. Trailing leg follows and comes down so that body returns to standing position facing location where it started.

VARIATIONS:

Can you keep your legs extended throughout?
Can you keep your legs in a wide *straddle?*
Can you finish with your arms overhead?
Can you pivot after finishing and do another *cartwheel?*

Inverted Balance

Performers who have completed the novice and intermediate inverted balance activities should have ample strength in the neck and ample balance to complete these advanced inverted activities, which culminate in the *headstand*. Do not require any performers to put weight on their head if they complain or show fear or anxiety. There are other movements that develop the important spatial orientation and integration of inner ear with muscle responses that can easily be substituted without putting weight on the neck. Some of these are on the low horizontal bar where the head hangs downward over the bar.

7.
- ☐ Introduced and understood
- ☐ Performs basic skill
- ☐ Conditioned response with variations

8.
- ☐ Introduced and understood
- ☐ Performs basic skill
- ☐ Conditioned response with variations

9.
- ☐ Introduced and understood
- ☐ Performs basic skill
- ☐ Conditioned response with variations

7. One Knee Up

DESCRIPTION:

Come to *tripod position*. Raise one knee off elbow and on up above hips.

VARIATIONS:

Can you wiggle your leg?
Can you change which knee is up?
Can you bend and straighten the free leg?
Can you come back to the *tripod position?*
Can you come down to an *all-fours position?*

8. Double Knee Up

DESCRIPTION:

Come to *tripod position*. Raise one knee up so that leg is bent. Then slowly bring other knee up beside first knee.

VARIATIONS:

Can you hold the position to the count of three?

Can you hold it to the count of six? How about ten?

Can you wiggle your legs and hips?

Can you wiggle your feet?

Who can touch their toes together, then heels?

Who can clap their feet together?

9. Headstand

DESCRIPTION:

Come to *tripod position*. Raise one leg up. Then slowly bring other leg up beside first so that both legs are extended upward.

VARIATIONS:

Can you hold your balance very still?

Can you hold it for six counts? (Do not stay on your head for any extended period of time—fifteen seconds would be a long time.)

Can you bend and straighten your knees?

Can you spread your feet sideways into a *straddle?* How far?

Can you bring one leg forward and one leg backward?

What other shapes can you make with your legs?

Can you come down slowly to a *straddle stand?* To an *all-fours position?*

Upright Agility

The advanced levels of upright agility require considerable power in the legs and dexterity of body. The performer should concentrate on completing the movement on the way upward so that coming down can be used to prepare for landing. However, in those variations where the performers are asked to execute a ¼ or a ½ twist as they land, the twist can be done on the descent phase of the jump. These same upright agility movements can be done on the springboard, and in fact learning them on the floor is a bit more difficult but a bit more safe than learning them on the springboard.

Caution: Safety requires that the performer land with at least a slight forward lean, bent hips, and bent knees. This precaution will help to avoid back injury.

7.
- ☐ Introduced and understood
- ☐ Performs basic skill
- ☐ Conditioned response with variations

8.
- ☐ Introduced and understood
- ☐ Performs basic skill
- ☐ Conditioned response with variations

9.
- ☐ Introduced and understood
- ☐ Performs basic skill
- ☐ Conditioned response with variations

7. Straddle Knee Touch

DESCRIPTION:
Jump upward and straddle legs forward and upward so that hands can touch knees. Quickly bring legs down to recover in *balanced landing position*.

VARIATIONS:
Can you point your toes toward the ceiling?
Can you point your toes straight out?
How high can you jump and touch your knees?
Can you turn your legs and feet a ¼ turn as you land?
Can you make a ¼ twist as you are going up for the knee touch?

8. Straddle Toe Touch

DESCRIPTION:

Jump upward and straddle legs forward and upward; simultaneously bend forward at waist and reach out to touch toes. Quickly return legs under body to recover in *balanced landing position.*

VARIATIONS:

How high can you leap?
Can you make a ¼ twist as you land?
Can you make a ¼ twist as you go up?

9. Pike Jump

DESCRIPTION:

Jump upward and, keeping legs straight, bring them forward and upward; simultaneously bend at waist and reach forward to touch ankles. Quickly return legs under body to recover in a *balanced landing position.*

VARIATIONS:

How high can you leap?
Can you keep your legs straight while they are up in front?
Caution: Be sure to bend them before you attempt the landing.
Can you make a ¼ twist as you are landing? Can you make a ½ twist?

Rolling Over Forward

Rolling now becomes a true joy. The feeling of completing 360 degrees of rotation in a continuous smooth turn and returning to a *balanced control position* is a great feeling of accomplishment. It is as though one has conquered space. With this activity mastered to the level of a conditioned response, the performer now begins to look for interesting maneuvers to execute during, before, and after the roll.

7.
- ☐ Introduced and understood
- ☐ Performs basic skill
- ☐ Conditioned response with variations

8.
- ☐ Introduced and understood
- ☐ Performs basic skill
- ☐ Conditioned response with variations

9.
- ☐ Introduced and understood
- ☐ Performs basic skill
- ☐ Conditioned response with variations

7. Forward Roll from Scale

DESCRIPTION:

Stand erect with good posture. Take all of weight on one leg; raise opposite leg into a *bent hip scale*. Bend forward at waist, reach down with both arms extended to mat, then lean into *forward roll*.

VARIATIONS:

Can you touch the mat with both hands and hold for a moment before you kick over into your *forward roll?*

Can you raise the free leg higher and bring the hands closer to the supporting foot?

Can you use your opposite leg as the supporting leg?

Can you hold the arms outward before reaching down to roll?

8. Step—Leap—Forward Roll

DESCRIPTION:

Begin three paces from end of mat. Step forward on one foot and leap off that foot to land on both feet just in front of mat. After you land on both feet lean forward, bend at waist, and reach down to *forward roll.*

VARIATIONS:

Can you pause just a moment after the leap and before the roll?

Can you make a smooth transition into the roll?

As you come out of the roll put one foot in front of the other. Can you cross your legs at the ankles as you rise out of the roll? And make a ½ turn to face the direction you were coming from?

As you come up out of the roll how high can you rise on one foot only?

Instead of a step and leap, can you make several hops on both feet before you reach down for the roll?

9. Reach Over—Forward Roll

DESCRIPTION:

Stand with a low obstacle between you and edge of mat. (Obstacle can be another child or some soft object but should be about one-half as high as the knees.) Then bend at knees and waist, reach over obstacle, and execute a *forward roll.*

VARIATIONS:

Can you raise one foot before your hands touch?

Can you raise the other foot before your hands touch?

Can you raise out of the roll with one foot in front of the other?

Can you raise out of the roll with your feet close together? Shoulder width apart? Even wider?

Do you have a variation of your own?

Rolling Over Backward

Teacher's Note: Abundant preparation is very important before any performer should attempt the *backward straddle roll* or the *backward roll*. The novice and intermediate activities for rolling over backward are very helpful. Rolling backward down an incline is a very helpful preparation for rolling over backward.

The novice and intermediate activities have prepared the performer with many of the patterns of rolling over backward and with some of the feelings and sensations in the inner ear. However, one of the more important feelings is yet to come—that of reaching back with the hands to take the weight off the neck. Once this skill is accomplished, the *backward roll* will be every bit as much fun as the *forward roll*.

7.
- ☐ Introduced and understood
- ☐ Performs basic skill
- ☐ Conditioned response with variations

8.
- ☐ Introduced and understood
- ☐ Performs basic skill
- ☐ Conditioned response with variations

9.
- ☐ Introduced and understood
- ☐ Performs basic skill
- ☐ Conditioned response with variations

7. Shoulder Balance

DESCRIPTION:

Sit on mat with knees bent. Hold hands in front with thumbs toward each other and palms of hands toward wall in front. Now, keeping thumbs inward toward each other, raise elbows as hands are brought back to shoulders with palms facing wall behind you. Rock back through *back rocker* and slightly farther so that palms of hands can be pressed against mat by your shoulders. Elbows and knees are in close proximity.

VARIATIONS:

Can you feel your hands press against the mat near your shoulders?

Can you raise and lower your legs in a pumping action? Does some of the weight come off your back when you pump your legs upward?

As your legs are pumping upward, simultaneously press against the mat with your hands to raise the shoulders slightly off the mat.

8. Backward Straddle Roll

DESCRIPTION:

Sit on mat with knees bent and arms up prepared to take the *shoulder balance* position. Rock back vigorously, straddle legs wide, and press hard on floor with palms of hands. Allow feet to take their place on mat and then press with hands and straighten arms to raise head off mat and complete the *backward straddle roll.*

VARIATIONS:

As you rock backward can you pull your legs over your head a little more vigorously?

Can you straddle your feet a little wider than your shoulders?

Can you start from a *squat* on your heels, then sit back into the *backward straddle roll?* Does the extra momentum help you?

9. Backward Roll

DESCRIPTION:

Start in *squat position,* sitting on heels with hands on mat. Sit back and continue rocking backward through *shoulder balance position.* Push with arms to raise head up and allow hips to continue overhead. Push weight onto feet and continue upward to standing position.

VARIATIONS:

Can you finish with your feet together?

Can you finish with your feet apart?

Can you start from standing, squat down, and continue through *backward roll?*

Can you finish on one foot only?

Advanced Springboard Activities

Forward Bouncing

Children should come to the advanced-level springboard activities with a good set of conditioned responses for bouncing and landing. The teacher should review some of the novice and intermediate activities for warm-up and as preparation for the advanced activities.

Maturation and Summer Growth: Over the summer, children may have changed in body, weight, and experience. Often children will have different leg length, arm length, and body weight when the new school year starts. These body changes need to be registered with the nervous system as it attempts to call upon previously programmed conditioned responses. Review of novice and intermediate skills will accomplish this for the child.

7.
- ☐ Introduced and understood
- ☐ Performs basic skill
- ☐ Conditioned response with variations

8.
- ☐ Introduced and understood
- ☐ Performs basic skill
- ☐ Conditioned response with variations

9.
- ☐ Introduced and understood
- ☐ Performs basic skill
- ☐ Conditioned response with variations

7. Straddle Leg Touch

DESCRIPTION:

Bounce off end of springboard and immediately bring legs outward and upward in a *bent hip straddle.* At the same time bend forward at hips and reach outward and down with arms and hands to touch legs in flight. Quickly return legs under body to recover in *landing position.*

VARIATIONS:

Can you touch your legs near the knees?

Can you land *on balance?* Can you hold the balance for three counts?

Can you touch your legs out past the knees? On the shins? On the ankles?

Can you point your toes outward and away from the body?

Can you touch the tops of your feet as the toes point outward?

8. Pike Bounce

DESCRIPTION:

Bounce off springboard and immediately bring legs forward and upward, holding them straight and together. Quickly return legs under body to recover in *landing position*.

TEACHER'S NOTE:

One technique for practicing the *pike bounce* is to stand on the floor and hold a cubie (bean bag) between the feet. Then attempt to throw the cubie forward with the feet.

VARIATIONS:

Can you land *on balance?*

Can you keep your legs straight as you are going up? **Caution:** Be sure to bend them as you land.

Can you raise your arms vigorously upward to get more height?

Can you make a ¼ turn as you land?

9. Pike Leg Touch

DESCRIPTION:

Bounce off springboard and immediately bring legs up in the *pike position*. Simultaneously bend forward at hips, lean shoulders out, and bring arms and hands down to touch legs in flight. Quickly return legs downward under body to recover in *landing position*.

VARIATIONS:

Can you land on balance? Can you touch your legs at the knees?

Can you keep your legs straight as you raise them up to touch your hands? **Caution:** Be sure to bend your legs as you take the *landing position*.

Can you touch out past your knees and on the shin?

Can you touch your legs at the ankles?

Can you point your toes out away from your body?

Can you touch the tops of your feet as you do the *pike leg touch?*

Twisting

During this series we combine rebounding with twisting. The bounce should not be very high. Review rebounding and twisting at the novice and intermediate levels.

7.
- ☐ Introduced and understood
- ☐ Performs basic skill
- ☐ Conditioned response with variations

8.
- ☐ Introduced and understood
- ☐ Performs basic skill
- ☐ Conditioned response with variations

9.
- ☐ Introduced and understood
- ☐ Performs basic skill
- ☐ Conditioned response with variations

7. Rebound

DESCRIPTION:

Take a very low bounce off springboard; anticipate landing on mat so that immediately upon touching mat you bounce upward again. Legs are firm but not straight on this *rebound* action.

VARIATIONS:

Can you take several *rebounds* after you land on the mat?

Can you rebound into a ¼ twist?

Can you rebound with ¼ twists until you have turned 360 degrees? **Note:** you do not want much forward motion when you are trying to twist.

Can you rebound into a ½ twist?

8. Reverse Stand—½ Twist Off

DESCRIPTION:

Stand on springboard near forward edge and then turn around to be facing in reverse direction. Landing mat will now be behind you. Twist your head and shoulders around to look back toward landing mat; then bounce off springboard and make a ½ twist to land facing forward.

VARIATIONS:

Can you hold your balance?

Can you bounce a little higher?

Can you rebound forward upon landing?

Can you rebound three times forward upon landing?

Can you rebound into a ¼ twist? A ½ twist?

9. ½ Twist On—½ Twist Off

DESCRIPTION:

Approach springboard with one or two steps. As you leap onto springboard make a ½ twist to land in a reverse stand; then bounce off springboard and continue with another ½ twist to land on mat facing the original direction.

VARIATIONS:

Can you make the two twists smoothly so that they seem like a continuous movement?

Can you land *on balance?* Can you hold the *landing position* for three counts?

Can you bounce a little higher coming off the springboard?

Can you do a *knee slapper* coming off the board? A *seat kicker?*

Can you rebound off the mat into some additional movement?

Rolling Sequence

The rolling sequence at the advanced level is a dynamic experience for the body. Children feel a great deal of accomplishment when they master these movements, which include an aerial movement followed by a rolling movement of 360 degrees and finishing back in a standing position. The kinesthetic sensations present somewhat of a symphony of input. This is a taste of gymnastics that will cause a few children to want to continue into the competitive programs.

Caution: It is important to review the novice and intermediate activities as a warm-up before launching into these advanced movements. It is especially important to emphasize landing on the feet prior to moving into the roll.

7. ☐ Introduced and understood
☐ Performs basic skill
☐ Conditioned response with variations

8. ☐ Introduced and understood
☐ Performs basic skill
☐ Conditioned response with variations

9. ☐ Introduced and understood
☐ Performs basic skill
☐ Conditioned response with variations

7. Pike Bounce—Forward Roll

DESCRIPTION:
Bounce from springboard into a *pike position*, recover to *landing position*, and then continue into a *forward roll*.

VARIATIONS:
Can you balance for two counts between the *pike* and the *forward roll*?
Can you land and move smoothly into the *forward roll*?
Can you execute a *pike leg touch* before the *forward roll*?
Can you execute a *pike ankle touch* before the *forward roll*?

8. Straddle Bounce—Forward Roll

DESCRIPTION:

Approach springboard with one or two steps. Bounce off springboard and into a *straddle bounce*. Recover to the *landing position* and pause for two counts. Then lean forward into a *forward roll*.

VARIATIONS:

Can you hold a good balance upon landing from the *straddle bounce?*

Can you move smoothly into the *forward roll?*

Can you execute a *straddle knee touch? Shin touch? Foot touch?*

Can you bounce a little higher on the *straddle bounce?*

Can you come out of the *forward roll* with one foot in front of the other?

What else can you do coming out of the *forward roll?*

9. ½ On—½ Off—Forward Roll

DESCRIPTION:

Approach springboard with one or two steps. When leaping onto springboard do a ½ turn to land on board in reverse stand, then continue off board with a ½ turn to land on mat facing original direction; pause for two counts and then lean into a *forward roll*.

VARIATIONS:

Can you raise your arms up overhead on the ½ turn off to get a high lift?

Can you land from the ½ turn off so that you are in good control and ready to move into the *forward roll?*

Can you do a *bunny hop* before the *forward roll?*

Can you come out of the *forward roll* with a ¼ turn?

What other variation can you do coming out of the *forward roll?*

With Table

The *forward roll* from the springboard onto the tumbling table gives the body the sensation of completing an aerial somersault. This is a very exhilarating feeling and definitely has a motivating effect on children. Children usually want to do this movement again and again. The movement turns the body 360 degrees with a "light on your feet" feeling.

Caution: The advanced-level activities require that the performer has previously mastered the novice and intermediate levels. Be sure to review the novice and intermediate skills.

7.
- ☐ Introduced and understood
- ☐ Performs basic skill
- ☐ Conditioned response with variations

8.
- ☐ Introduced and understood
- ☐ Performs basic skill
- ☐ Conditioned response with variations

9.
- ☐ Introduced and understood
- ☐ Performs basic skill
- ☐ Conditioned response with variations

7. Bounce to Tuck

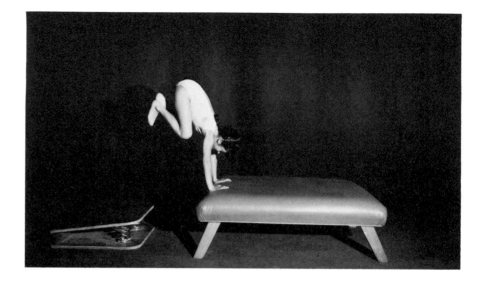

DESCRIPTION:

Place springboard about 10 inches from end of tumbling table. Stand on springboard, bend over, and put hands on table. While arms support body, bounce hips up and pull knees close to chest. Return feet to original place on springboard.

VARIATIONS:

Can you bounce your feet into the air several consecutive times off the springboard?

Can you push with firm arms and look down between your hands when your hips go up in the air?

Can you pull knees and feet up to a *tuck* and then quickly return them to the springboard?

TEACHER'S NOTE:

This is the leg and hip action that will be necessary to successfully complete the next movement, the *forward roll* over the table.

8. Forward Roll over Tumbling Table   9. Roll On—Roll After

DESCRIPTION:

Place springboard comfortably close to end of table. Stand on springboard with hands on tumbling table and prepare to bounce hips over head. Take a good beat on board and bounce hips over head and execute a *forward roll* on tumbling table so that you finish sitting on table. Lean forward to a stand to finish the movement.

VARIATIONS:

Can you approach the springboard and immediately bounce into a *forward roll?*

Can you rebound out of the *forward roll?*

Can you rebound into a ¼ twist?

Can you rebound into a ½ twist?

DESCRIPTION:

Place springboard a comfortable distance from tumbling table (about 10 inches for young children, farther for elementary school ages and adults). Place hands on tumbling table and then bounce into a *forward roll* onto table. As feet come to mat, lean forward off tumbling table and into another *forward roll.*

VARIATIONS:

Do the two rolls make you dizzy? Can you pause between the rolls?

Can you jump upward between the rolls?

Can you do two ½ twists between the rolls?

What variation would you like to do?

Advanced Low Horizontal Bar Activities

Swinging Under

The experiences from the novice and intermediate levels of activity are prerequisite to success at the advanced level. Be sure to review these activities as warm-ups before beginning the advanced activities. At the advanced level the timing becomes ever more important. Movements require that actions come at just the right time in order to achieve success.

7.
- ☐ Introduced and understood
- ☐ Performs basic skill
- ☐ Conditioned response with variations

8.
- ☐ Introduced and understood
- ☐ Performs basic skill
- ☐ Conditioned response with variations

9.
- ☐ Introduced and understood
- ☐ Performs basic skill
- ☐ Conditioned response with variations

7. Squat—Kick over Rope

CAUTION:

Make sure rope is far enough away from the bar so that the children will not hit their head, yet close enough that the children can get over and come to a stand (about 24–30 inches).

DESCRIPTION:

Facing bar take *double over grip* and squat so that seat is near heels. Kick one foot up in front as if taking a giant step, bring other foot up with first, and swing out over a rope held about 6 inches above mat. Bring feet down and push hips upward in an arch to lift body beyond rope to a standing position.

NOTE: A foam-rubber pipe insulator is firm enough to be held by one assistant and may thus replace the rope.

VARIATIONS:

Can you go over if the rope is raised to 8 inches? Ten inches?
Can you land in a standing position?
Do you lean back away from the rope before you start? Does that give you more swing?
Can you go over if the rope is raised to 14 inches?

8. Underswing over Line

CAUTION:

The line should be far enough from the bar that the performers do not hit their head on the bar as they swing under. The arms should be kept straight and the head should not be lifted upward until the shoulders have passed under the bar.

DESCRIPTION:

Stand facing bar with feet near line between supports, take *double over grip*, and lean back away from bar. Bring one leg up near bar and immediately push off other leg, bring it up to join first, and swing out over line on mat beyond bar. Bring feet down and arch hips to finish in *balanced landing position*.

VARIATIONS:

Can you get both legs near the bar as you swing under?
Who can swing under and arch out smoothly?
Who can land *on balance* and hold it for three counts?
Who can begin the underswing by jumping off both feet and raising both at the same time?

9. Underswing over Rope

CAUTION:

The rope should be held out away from the bar so that the student has room to swing under the bar and over the rope without hitting the head on the bar. The arms should be held straight until the shoulders have passed under the bar and beyond the bar supports.

DESCRIPTION:

Stand facing bar with feet near line between supports, take *double over grip*, and lean back away from bar. Bring one leg up near bar, then push off and bring other leg up by first; swing under bar and out over rope. Bring legs down and arch hips to come to a *balanced landing position*.

VARIATIONS:

Can you go over a rope held 12 inches above the mat? How about 18 inches? How high can you go and still land safely? (Move rope upward in small increments.)

Can you twist your legs as you go up and over to execute a ½ twist and land facing the point at which you started?

Support above Bar

At the advanced level children develop a greater sense of balance. Experience on the bar is more important to success than strength in these activities. The body must respond to very slight changes in the center of gravity in order to keep the trunk balanced above the very thin bar.

As with other sequential skills, it is important to review the novice and intermediate activities.

7. ☐ Introduced and understood
☐ Performs basic skill
☐ Conditioned response with variations

8. ☐ Introduced and understood
☐ Performs basic skill
☐ Conditioned response with variations

9. ☐ Introduced and understood
☐ Performs basic skill
☐ Conditioned response with variations

7. One-Leg Balance

DESCRIPTION:

From *front support*, put one leg over bar so that you can sit on that leg. Return leg back to *front support*.

VARIATIONS:

Can you balance for five counts?

Can you put the opposite leg over the bar?

While sitting on one leg can you raise one hand up and balance?

Do you bend your knee when you raise the leg over the bar?

Can you keep your leg straight when you put it over the bar?

While in the balanced position, can you put the raised hand outside the leg and onto the bar and then raise the opposite hand?

8. Sitting Toe Touch

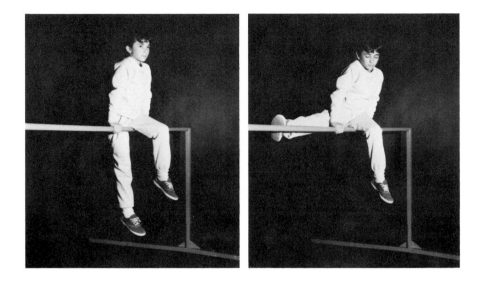

DESCRIPTION:

From *front support,* put one leg over bar to sit on that leg. Then put hand over that leg and onto bar with *under grip* (thumb forward). Raise other leg to touch toes on bar.

TEACHER'S NOTE:

The *under grip* is especially important on the next skill in this progression, *alternate legs over.* Therefore, it is important to develop the kinesthetic feeling of the *under grip* while learning the *sitting toe touch.*

VARIATIONS:

Can you touch your toe to the top of the bar?

Can you put your foot on top of the bar and balance there?

Can you put the other leg over and touch the opposite toe?

9. Alternate Legs Over

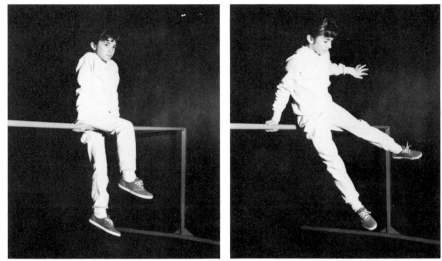

DESCRIPTION:

From *front support,* put one leg over bar to sit on that leg. Then put hand outside that leg and take bar with *under grip* (thumb forward). Lean shoulders over supporting leg and raise other leg over bar; as it comes over bar, allow body to drop down to *balanced landing position,* facing slightly toward supporting hand. Hand with *under grip* will still be on bar to steady landing.

VARIATIONS:

Can you raise the second leg over and smoothly drop down?

Can you bend the leg straight as it comes over the bar?

After the second leg is clear of the bar can you take a ¼ turn toward the supporting hand as you jump down?

Who can begin with the opposite lcg?

Who can keep the legs straight as they go over the bar?

Who can maintain a rhythm as they put first one, then the other leg over?

Grip Changes and Turning

At the advanced level we begin to execute movements in which weight is momentarily on the arms and hands. This requires previous development of arm strength and a delicate sensitivity to balance. These prerequisites will have been achieved if students have mastered the novice and intermediate activities.

7.
- ☐ Introduced and understood
- ☐ Performs basic skill
- ☐ Conditioned response with variations

8.
- ☐ Introduced and understood
- ☐ Performs basic skill
- ☐ Conditioned response with variations

9.
- ☐ Introduced and understood
- ☐ Performs basic skill
- ☐ Conditioned response with variations

7. Single Leg Over—Hip Swivel

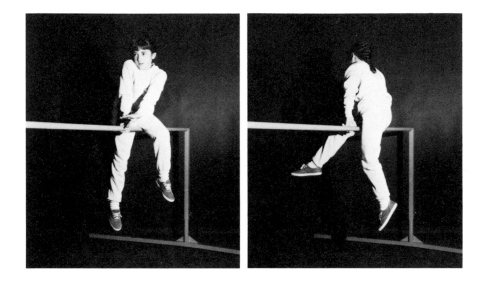

DESCRIPTION:

Come to *front support* with *mixed grip*. Place leg by over-grip hand over bar to sitting. Slide the under-grip hand between legs. Now twist shoulders toward under-grip hand; this will allow you to turn so as to place over-grip hand past other hand and onto bar facing the opposite direction (both hands are facing the same way and will be in an over grip). Now swivel hips so that weight is shifted to opposite leg and simultaneously turn shoulders to face opposite direction.

VARIATIONS:

Who can make the movement smoothly?

Who can recover from the *swivel* to a *front support* facing the opposite direction?

Who can swivel back to the opposite direction without moving the hands?

Who can start with the opposite leg?

8. Single Leg Cuts

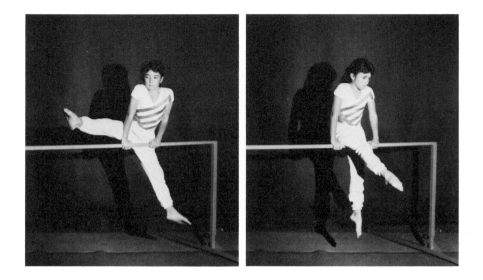

9. Single Leg Over—½ Turn

DESCRIPTION:

Take *front support* with *double over grip.* Lean toward one arm as you swing opposite leg up and over bar. Leaning will allow you to raise hand on side of raised leg. As leg comes over bar, place free hand over leg to a support on bar; by slight twisting of hips allow leg to swing in front of body. As swinging leg returns, allow it to cut again under hand and return over bar back to *front support position.* Repeat using opposite leg.

VARIATIONS:

Do you lean toward the supporting hand? Smooth action cannot occur without this lean.

Can you make the cut smooth? Can you keep your leg straight?

Do you twist your hips on the leg swing?

Can you follow one leg cut with another from the opposite side?

Can you make both leg cuts a part of one smooth rhythm?

DESCRIPTION:

Take *mixed grip* and jump to *front support position.* Lean toward over-grip hand and bring opposite leg over bar and under hand with under grip. Lean on under-grip arm and raise opposite leg over bar. Simultaneously, shoulders turn toward under-grip hand to face in opposite direction as free hand reaches over support hand to a *double over grip.* Body will now be in a *front support* facing opposite direction.

VARIATIONS:

Can you prepare for the turn while sitting on one leg in the original direction?

Do you lean over the support arm when you make your turn? Do you fall to the mat when you do not lean over the support arm?

Can you change your grip and make all turns in the opposite direction? Does one direction seem easier than the other? Practice the easiest direction until it gets smooth.

Around the Bar

The *back pull over* requires strength in the arms, strength in the abdomen, and the proper timing of muscle contractions. The *leg curl* and the *assisted back pull over* will help get children prepared for this skill.

7. ☐ Introduced and understood
☐ Performs basic skill
☐ Conditioned response with variations

8. ☐ Introduced and understood
☐ Performs basic skill
☐ Conditioned response with variations

9. ☐ Introduced and understood
☐ Performs basic skill
☐ Conditioned response with variations

7. Leg Curl

DESCRIPTION:

Stand close to bar with *double over grip.* Bring chest close to bar, keep chin above bar, elbows bent, and then raise knees in front of face to curl around bar. Resist gravity as it attempts to pull your chin down below bar. Hold momentarily.

VARIATIONS:

Who can hold the *leg curl* for three counts? How about four counts? Five?

Can you keep your chin above the bar?

Can you get both your chin and your knees above the bar?

Can you touch the bar with your legs?

Can you keep your elbows bent and look over the bar at your knees?

8. Assisted Back Pull Over

DESCRIPTION:

Performer hangs below bar and lifts one leg up to partner. Partner holds leg up as performer does a *leg curl* with free leg until bar slips into hips. Partner puts other leg over bar and helps performer raise shoulders to *front support.*

VARIATIONS:

Can you watch your knee until it is over the bar?

After the *pull over* can you lift your head and shoulders to a *front support* without help?

Do you put the bar deep into the crease of your hip and partly up on your stomach? This extra little pull will help you get to a *front support.*

After the *pull over,* can you lower down to a *front roll?*

9. Back Pull Over

DESCRIPTION:

Start with elbows bent, bar about chin height and close to chest. Execute *leg curl* and continue pulling legs over bar until bar comes into hips. Raise head and shoulders to *front support.*

VARIATIONS:

Can you kick one leg up over the bar, then pull the other one over? Which is easier, leading with one leg or raising both legs at once?

Can you stop in a *front support,* then *front roll* down?

Rotating under the Bar

These advanced movements give children a great sense of accomplishment because they will have learned to trust their grip to defy gravity as they swing under and up onto the bar. The sense of timing required for success in the *single leg uprise* is very precise as is the sense of balance. These are among the favorite activities of children.

7. ☐ Introduced and understood
   ☐ Performs basic skill
   ☐ Conditioned response with variations

8. ☐ Introduced and understood
   ☐ Performs basic skill
   ☐ Conditioned response with variations

9. ☐ Introduced and understood
   ☐ Performs basic skill
   ☐ Conditioned response with variations

7. Single Leg Swing Back

DESCRIPTION:

While in *front support* place one leg over bar and bend knee. Allow elbows to bend and hips to lower until bar slides into bent knee, then continue swinging backward until you are hanging under bar with one knee hooked over bar and other leg held up in front. Disengage leg from bar and lower to a sitting position.

VARIATIONS:

Can you swing back smoothly?

Do you feel sure that your hands will hold you?

When you put the leg over the bar, bring it under the arm so that it is *between the two arms*. Now can you do the *single leg swing back?*

When you swing back can you keep your arms a bit straighter?

Can you keep your arms straight when you swing back? Does this make you have a bigger swing?

8. Double Leg Swing Back

DESCRIPTION:

From *front support position*, put one leg over bar and sit on bar. Bring other leg over bar and sit. Now bend elbows and let seat drop behind bar and slowly turn upside down. Allow legs to continue on over to floor in *skin the cat* fashion.

VARIATIONS:

Can you lean chest down to touch thighs before falling back?

Can you hang upside down and know where you are before bringing your feet to the floor?

After coming to a hang can you straighten your legs and hold *basket position*?

9. Single Leg Uprise

DESCRIPTION:

From *front support position* bring one leg forward and cut under hand to sit with leg between arms. Execute *single leg swing back* with arms straight and free leg swinging upward in front. Shoulders will swing downward and on past bar supports. As shoulders swing back under bar supports, force free leg downward and pull hands downward to bring shoulders upward over hands until position of support above bar is regained.

TEACHER'S NOTE:

Students tend to bend the elbows and bring the chin to the bar before a good back swing has been attained. Success comes when students learn to swing outward with straight arms, then take a good swing backward with the free leg forced downward *before* they pull the shoulders and chin over the hands.

CAUTION:

A vigorous uprise can take the student too far and cause him or her to fall forward over the bar. The teacher should stand in front of the bar by the student until both student and teacher are confident.

Hip Casting

Learning a successful *cast* requires that the shoulders and arms be strong and that the performer have a good sense of balance through the arms. Each movement should be done from a *front support* on the mat numerous times before it is done on the bar. This will help the performer learn how much to lean the shoulders forward of the hands to maintain good balance.

7.
- ☐ Introduced and understood
- ☐ Performs basic skill
- ☐ Conditioned response with variations

8.
- ☐ Introduced and understood
- ☐ Performs basic skill
- ☐ Conditioned response with variations

9.
- ☐ Introduced and understood
- ☐ Performs basic skill
- ☐ Conditioned response with variations

7. Cast to Tuck

DESCRIPTION:

Take *front support* with *double over grip.* Allow legs a slight swing forward and backward for timing. Then swing forward again and on second swing backward vigorously lift legs upward behind body as in *seat kicker;* then quickly bring knees up under body in *tuck position.* Extend legs and fall to mat in a *balanced landing position* with hands still on bar.

VARIATIONS:

How high can you raise your legs behind your body before you begin the *tuck?*

Can you pause just a moment at the height of the *cast?*

Can you bring your legs in so that they reach the *tuck position* just at the top of the *cast?*

Can you touch the bar with your toes?

Can you control your landing on the mat?

8. Cast to Pike

DESCRIPTION:

From *front support* swing legs upward behind as toward the *seat kicker.* Then quickly push seat upward, round back, and keeping legs straight bring them toward hands. Allow body to fall to *balanced landing position* with hands still on bar.

VARIATIONS:

Can you keep your arms straight?
Can you push your hips higher than your head?
Can you bring your toes close to the bar?
Can you touch the bar with your toes?

9. Cast to Straddle

DESCRIPTION:

From *front support* swing legs upward behind. Then quickly push seat upward, straddle legs, and bring toes toward bar.

VARIATIONS:

Can you keep your legs straight?
Can you push your hips as high as your head?
Can you touch the bar with your toes?
Can you momentarily put the soles of your feet on top of the bar?

Advanced Tumbling Table Activities

Vaulting Over

Vaulting at the advanced level requires increasing confidence in the arms as a means of support. The run and flight involved with vaulting makes it a favorite activity of young children.

7. ☐ Introduced and understood
   ☐ Performs basic skill
   ☐ Conditioned response with variations

8. ☐ Introduced and understood
   ☐ Performs basic skill
   ☐ Conditioned response with variations

9. ☐ Introduced and understood
   ☐ Performs basic skill
   ☐ Conditioned response with variations

7. Bounce to Tuck

DESCRIPTION:

Place hands on level table. Then bounce hips up and lean on arms. As hips bounce up, quickly pull knees to chest. Recover to *balanced landing position.*

VARIATIONS:

Can you make three quick bounces?

Can you touch your knees to your chest?

How high can you bounce your hips?

Can you bounce your hips up higher than your head and shoulders?

8. Bounce On, Then Over

DESCRIPTION:

Place hands to one side of level table. Bounce up onto table; then bounce feet on over table.

VARIATIONS:

Do you have to move your hands before bouncing your feet off the other side?

Can your hands reach past the center of the table?

Can you turn the opposite direction as you go over?

Can you bounce over in one direction, then return in the opposite direction?

9. Bounce Over

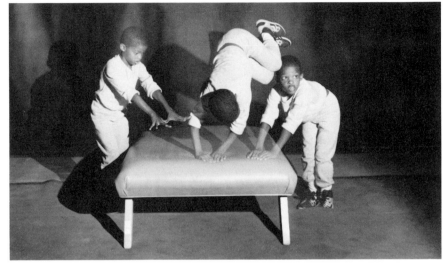

DESCRIPTION:

Run up to level table and bounce both feet simultaneously from one side of table to the other while arms support body in the air.

VARIATIONS:

Can you land *on balance?*

Can you pull your knees to your chest as you go over?

Can you land facing the direction from which you came?

Who takes their feet around the right side of the table? Who goes around the left?

Rolling Forward

No activities in Developmental Gymnastics feel more like tumbling than rolling forward on the level table. The sensation is that of an aerial *somersault*. The table holds the back while the body goes through 360 degrees of rotation and returns to the standing position so very easily.

Caution: There is a danger of overly enthusiastic children reaching out too far and going over the table instead of rolling on the top of the table. The hands must be placed near the close edge of the table as the performer begins the roll.

7.
- ☐ Introduced and understood
- ☐ Performs basic skill
- ☐ Conditioned response with variations

8.
- ☐ Introduced and understood
- ☐ Performs basic skill
- ☐ Conditioned response with variations

9.
- ☐ Introduced and understood
- ☐ Performs basic skill
- ☐ Conditioned response with variations

7. Forward Roll—Level

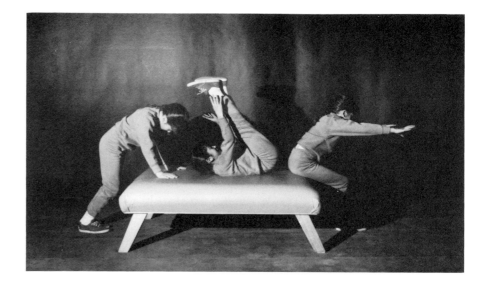

CAUTION:

An overly enthusiastic student can easily reach out too far and go over the table instead of rolling on top of the table. Caution the students to place their hands near the close edge of the table so that they will not run out of room to roll.

DESCRIPTION:

Stand back about 5 feet from level table with its longest side leading away from you. Take a step and then bounce off both feet, place hands on table near close edge, and forward roll on top of table. Complete roll by standing up beyond far edge of table.

VARIATIONS:

Can you bounce your hips over your head smoothly?

Can you duck your head under to make your back round and roll smoothly?

Can you finish the roll and then leap up?

Can you follow the leap with another roll?

8. Straddle Roll—Level

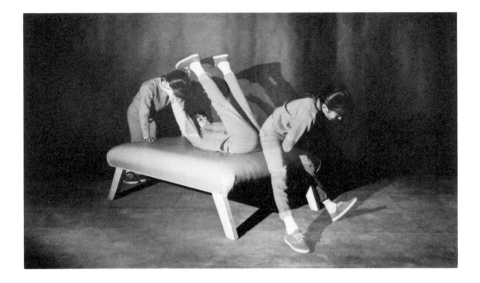

DESCRIPTION:

Approach level table, bounce into a *forward roll* on top of table; then straddle legs so as to finish roll in a *straddle stand.*

VARIATIONS:

Who can lean forward in the *straddle stand?*

Who can push off the table at the finish with hands between the legs?

Can you roll into a *straddle stand* without pushing with your hands?

Can you lean forward from the *straddle stand* to a *forward roll?* How about another *straddle roll?*

9. Pike Roll—Level

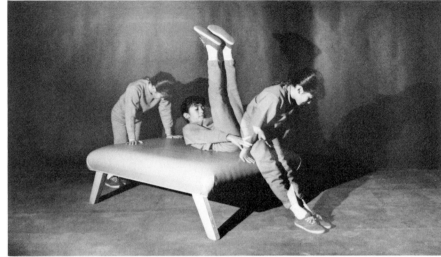

DESCRIPTION:

Approach table and bounce into a *forward roll.* Keep legs straight, lean forward, and push off table with hands at sides of hips to come to a stand with legs still straight.

VARIATIONS:

Can you raise to a stand with legs still straight?

Can you bend one knee and keep the other one straight?

Does it help to push with the hands?

Can you lean forward until your chest almost touches your legs?

Rolling Backward

This series may be the most difficult of the Developmental Gymnastics program. To execute the *backward roll* on a level surface the arms must reach back and the hands must press against the table to lift the body up and over the head and neck. This is difficult because the arms must push against a surface that the eyes cannot see. This feels like pushing something away from your back.

Caution: It is very important that the novice and intermediate activities for rolling backward be mastered prior to attempting the advanced program.

7. □ Introduced and understood
□ Performs basic skill
□ Conditioned response with variations

8. □ Introduced and understood
□ Performs basic skill
□ Conditioned response with variations

9. □ Introduced and understood
□ Performs basic skill
□ Conditioned response with variations

7. Straddle Back Roll

DESCRIPTION:

Sit on edge of slanted table with long side extended behind back. Raise hands, then elbows; push with legs and roll backward vigorously. Quickly straddle legs wide to take weight off hips and push hard against table surface with hands. Finish in *straddle stand.*

VARIATIONS:

Can you begin standing with table behind you, then sit down to *straddle back roll?*

Can you hold the *straddle stand* with your arms out wide?

Can you get out of the *straddle stand* finish by placing your hands on the table and jumping to a standing position?

8. Backward Roll

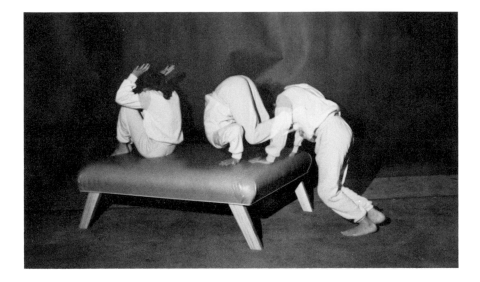

DESCRIPTION:

Sit on edge of level table with long axis extending away from you. Lift hands and elbows; roll vigorously backward and execute *backward roll* so that feet come over table and continue on to mat; finish in standing position.

VARIATIONS:

Can you push against the table with your hands?

Do you extend your legs slightly to help get your hips over your head?

Can you land with your feet together?

Can you land with one foot behind the other?

Who can hold their legs straight? What would you call this? (Answer: *piked back roll.*)

9. Back Roll, Then . . .

DESCRIPTION:

Sit on level table and execute *back roll*. After completing roll to a stand, leap upward with a ½ turn and execute a *forward roll* on mats.

VARIATIONS:

After completing the roll over the table can you sit down and complete a *back roll* on the mats?

Can you execute a *straddle back roll* over the level table and then from the *straddle stand* sit back into a *straddle back roll* on the mat?

What other variation of two or more rolls can you do using the level table?

Advanced Beam Activities

Balancing on the Level Beam

Challenges are added to the task of balancing at the advanced level. These new challenges require an even-greater sensitivity to the kinesthetic sensations and a very rapid response.

Floor Work: These movements should be practiced on the floor before getting on the beam. This will allow children to become very familiar with the pattern before they are required to add the balancing requirement.

7.
- ☐ Introduced and understood
- ☐ Performs basic skill
- ☐ Conditioned response with variations

8.
- ☐ Introduced and understood
- ☐ Performs basic skill
- ☐ Conditioned response with variations

9.
- ☐ Introduced and understood
- ☐ Performs basic skill
- ☐ Conditioned response with variations

7. Cross Over

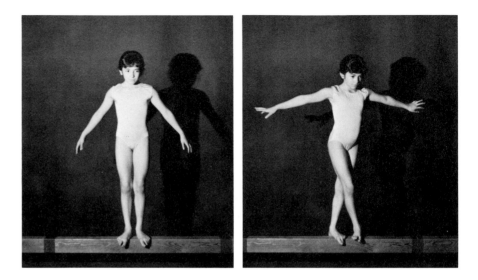

DESCRIPTION:
Stand crossways on beam. Bring one foot across and over other; then put weight on this foot and bring second foot back to standing position.

VARIATIONS:
Can you alternate crossing first right over left, then left over right?

Can you cross one foot behind the other?

Can you cross in one direction only to walk down the beam?

Can you cross behind in one direction only to walk down the beam?

8. Jump Switch

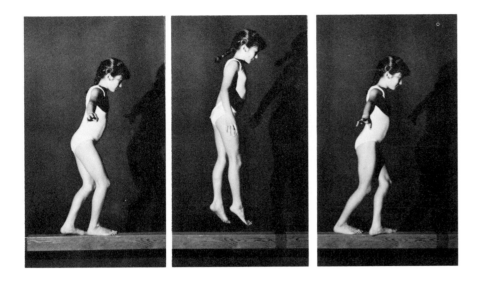

DESCRIPTION:

Balance facing along beam with one foot in front of other. Jump upward just enough to quickly switch places with feet.

VARIATIONS:

Do you sometimes move just one foot?

Can you move both feet?

Can you switch back and forth two times quickly? Three times?

Notice what you are doing with your arms. Can your arms take different positions? What position do you like most?

9. Twist-Jump

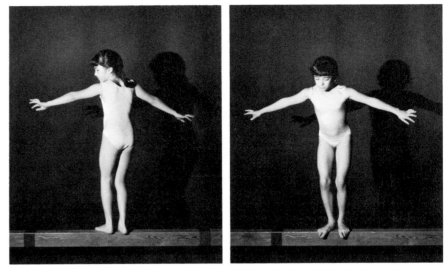

DESCRIPTION:

Balance crossways on beam. Turn head and shoulders and look behind. Then jump upward just enough to quickly bring feet around to where you are looking.

VARIATIONS:

Can you regain your balance in the new direction?

Can you twist and jump again back to your original direction?

Can you twist in the opposite direction? It this more difficult or is it easier?

Vaulting on the Level Beam

At the advanced level the beam is raised above the knees to the level of the thigh or near the waist. The beam at this level more nearly represents a fence or obstacle to be negotiated.

Any time children have difficulty succeeding with a new skill, the best solution is to review and give more attention to the previous skills in that series.

7.
☐ Introduced and understood
☐ Performs basic skill
☐ Conditioned response with variations

8.
☐ Introduced and understood
☐ Performs basic skill
☐ Conditioned response with variations

9.
☐ Introduced and understood
☐ Performs basic skill
☐ Conditioned response with variations

7. Step Through

DESCRIPTION:

Stand close with beam crossways in front. Place one hand on beam; then opposite foot is raised and placed so as to step onto beam. By supporting weight on hand and foot, lift hips so that body is off floor and balanced on beam. Now bring trailing knee and foot between body and beam and step through to land standing on opposite side of beam.

VARIATIONS:

Can you pause for a moment balanced on your hand and foot?
Can you use the opposite hand and foot for support?
Can you step through a little faster?

8. High Barrel Roll

DESCRIPTION:

Stand crossways to beam at intermediate height (about height of thigh) and back away about one large step. Take a step toward beam, place hands in *palm-to-palm grip* with hand corresponding to leading foot on near side of beam. Then kick trailing leg up and over beam to land on opposite side. Other leg follows as you continue turning and walk away.

VARIATIONS:

Can you step and kick over the beam smoothly?
Can you start a little farther from the beam?
Can you take two steps before the *barrel roll?*
Can you turn at the finish so as to walk away from the beam?

9. High Kangaroo Hop

DESCRIPTION:

With hands on beam in *palm-to-palm grip,* bounce hips and legs up and over beam to opposite side.

VARIATIONS:

Does it help you to take a small preparatory bounce for timing?
Can you bounce over and then back?
Can you bounce over and back two times?

Balancing on the Slanted Beam

At the advanced level added challenges make balancing a more complex skill. Children must learn to balance while concentrating on other tasks. This forces the balancing responses to the conditioned level and makes them more a part of our spontaneous physical capacity.

7. Ball Carry

DESCRIPTION:

While walking up slanted beam, carry a ball in your hands.

VARIATIONS:

Can you see where you will land when you jump down?
Can you jump down safely and *on balance?*
Can you roll the ball from one hand to the other?
Can you pass the ball behind your back as you walk?
Can you pass the ball under one leg as you walk?

7. ☐ Introduced and understood
☐ Performs basic skill
☐ Conditioned response with variations

8. ☐ Introduced and understood
☐ Performs basic skill
☐ Conditioned response with variations

9. ☐ Introduced and understood
☐ Performs basic skill
☐ Conditioned response with variations

8. Ball Toss

CAUTION:

Children should pitch and catch the ball on the floor before they get on the beam. If this is a difficult task on the floor, it should not be attempted on the beam. Catching a ball requires that the eyes be distracted momentarily from the beam and would be dangerous for the child who could not do both skills very well.

DESCRIPTION:

Carry a ball as you walk up slanted beam. Stop; carefully toss ball and catch it. Then continue walking.

VARIATIONS:

Can you keep your balance as you toss and catch?
Can you toss the ball a little higher?
Can you toss the ball to a friend before jumping down?
Can you toss the ball from one hand to the other?

9. Turn While Walking

DESCRIPTION:

While walking on slanted beam, pivot and turn to walk back down. Then pivot and turn to walk back up.

VARIATIONS:

Can you squat before you pivot?
Can you carry a ball as you make your turns?
Can you slide upward sideways, pivot, then slide down?

Vaulting on the Slanted Beam

The slanted beam allows a child to place his or her hands at the most comfortable height because every height is immediately available. Probably the best height to experiment with is the height of the thigh. After trying at that height a few times, children should naturally gravitate up or down to the position that is most comfortable to them. In this case lower is not necessarily easier. Reaching down too low puts more weight on the arms and tends to make the children feel that they are being pushed over on their nose.

When children master these activities they will have an added confidence in their ability to negotiate obstacles and handle their body out of doors.

7.
- ☐ Introduced and understood
- ☐ Performs basic skill
- ☐ Conditioned response with variations

8.
- ☐ Introduced and understood
- ☐ Performs basic skill
- ☐ Conditioned response with variations

9.
- ☐ Introduced and understood
- ☐ Performs basic skill
- ☐ Conditioned response with variations

7. Knee Balance

DESCRIPTION:
Stand beside beam facing high end. Place hands on beam in *palm-to-palm grip.* Now place knee closest to beam on beam and lift other leg off floor. This is the *knee balance.*

VARIATIONS:
Can you raise the free leg high behind your back?
Can you hold your free foot out to the side?
Can you hold the balance position for 5 seconds?
Can you approach from the opposite side and balance on the other knee?

8. Squat Balance

DESCRIPTION:

Stand beside beam facing high end. Place hands on beam in *palm-to-palm grip*. Now place foot closest to beam on beam with knee tucked up almost between elbows. Then lift other foot up and place behind first. The body is now in a *squat balance position*.

VARIATIONS:

Can you hold this position for 5 seconds?
Can you raise one foot up in the air behind the body?
Can you approach from the opposite side of the beam?

9. Squat Mount

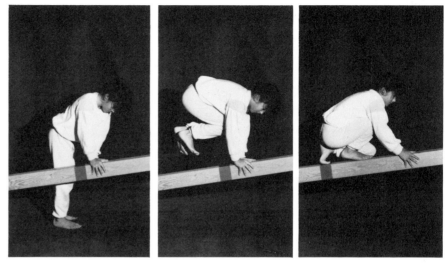

DESCRIPTION:

Stand beside beam facing high end. Place hands in *palm-to-palm grip*. Now bounce hips upward as in the *tuck bounce* and land in a *squat position* on beam with one foot slightly in front of other. This is the *squat mount*.

VARIATIONS:

Can you put your hands at a higher place on the beam?
Can you bounce higher before you land on the beam?
Can you switch the positions of the feet?
Can you approach the beam from the opposite direction?
Which side feels most natural?

5. Enrichment Activities for Fun and Show

As children accomplish each new motor pattern they seem very excited and happy. They want to experience the feelings over and over again and play with the movement patterns in a variety of situations. Children are eager to show their new skills to their friends, teachers, and parents.

This chapter offers just a few of the hundreds of ways in which children can enjoy these new skills. The activities described here can be used to add variety to the regular physical activity period, and they also form the basis for a Developmental Gymnastics show, which gives the children a chance to present their skills to family and community.

All Together

Once children can control their bodies well enough to execute a movement pattern, they encounter an additional challenge when they perform according to the instructor's command. The teacher should have the children execute almost every movement they learn in an "all together" group fashion. This requires that the children listen as well as perform. For the children to act together, the teacher must give some type of preparatory signal, such as a strong "Readyyy . . ." In this way the children can anticipate when the action should start.

1. All right, now that all of you can do the *tip over*, let's see if you can do it all together. On your hands and knees, head down, readyyy . . . Go!

2. Now that you can do the *back shoulder roll*, let's all try to do it at the same time. Sit down, readyyy . . . Go!

3. Get ready for the *forward roll.* Everyone standing, facing your mat, readyyy . . . Go!

Two in a Row

After children have good control over movements, such as the *forward roll, back shoulder roll, barrel roll,* and so on, several mats can be put together and the children can try Two in a Row.

1. Now that you can do a *forward roll*, can you do two in a row?
   Do you stand up tall between each roll?
   Can you do two without standing between them?
   How fast can you go?
   Does it make you dizzy?

2. How about the *back shoulder roll;* can you do two of those in a row?
   Can you hold one foot off the ground the whole time?

3. Can you do two *barrel rolls* in a row?

4. What else can you do two in a row?

Dominoes

If children can do a movement well, they like to use it in a domino line. The children are in line with their knees on the edge of the mat. The child at one end falls to the mat. The second child in line falls, then the next child, and so on, as though one domino were knocking the others down. After some practice the children become more aware of the visual and auditory cues and the pattern becomes smoother.

A strong preparatory command gets the children ready, but there should be no loud starting command because it would cause all to fall at once. The starting command is made by quietly calling the first child by name.

The *front fall* (falling from *knee stand* to stomach by catching with the arms) is a good movement to begin with. Once this is mastered, children like to use the *forward roll*, *back shoulder roll*, *full twist*, and many others.

Movement Story

Can you tell a story with movement? Here is one to try.

1. There was once a very small seed.

2. The seed was planted in fertile ground. The rains came, and the seed began slowly to grow.

3. And it grew and it grew and it grew until it became a great, tall tree with branches spread wide.

4. One day a lumberjack came along and said, "What fine lumber this tree will make." So he went chop, chop, chop. "Tim . . . ber . . . ," he cried, as it fell to the ground.

5. The branches were trimmed.

6. The logs were then rolled down the mountain to the mill, which was only a short distance away.

7. "How beautiful this wood is," said the miller. "It should be used for something nice." So some of the wood was used to make rocking chairs.

8. Some of it was made into sturdy benches.

9. Some of it was made into hat racks and coat racks.

10. And some of it was made into wagons that carried the products and helped the people of the land.

Wheelbarrow

Children always seem to enjoy helping each other. In doing the Wheelbarrow, each child has a partner. One partner, the "wheelbarrow," gets on hands and knees on a mat. The feet are raised up to be accessible "handles" for the "driver." The other partner, the driver, stands behind the wheelbarrow.

1. Wheelbarrow

CAUTION:

The "driver" does *not* push the wheelbarrow. The driver holds the wheelbarrow up and pretends to drive but does not actually push the other child.

DESCRIPTION:

Driver reaches down, takes hold of feet, and slowly lifts wheelbarrow up so that knees do not touch mat. Driver does not move but keeps feet in place and helps partner balance on arms. Now slowly let wheelbarrow back down to mat. Switch places.

VARIATIONS:

Can the wheelbarrow move the hands a little wider without losing balance? A little closer?

Can the wheelbarrow take a "step" to one side? To the other?

Can the wheelbarrow balance to the count of five? Ten?

2. Empty and Fill

DESCRIPTION:

While driver holds wheelbarrow up, wheelbarrow makes legs and body stiff and straight. To empty wheelbarrow, allow tummy to sag and look upward toward ceiling with arms kept straight. To fill wheelbarrow, slowly raise hips upward until they are higher than head. Slowly lower partner to mat. Switch places.

VARIATIONS:

How full can you fill your wheelbarrow *without* dumping it over?

Can you keep your legs straight while you fill it up?

Can you bend your knees?

3. Crazy Driver

DESCRIPTION:

Driver holds friend in wheelbarrow position. Wheelbarrow spreads feet for stability; driver holds feet at sides against hips. Wheelbarrow then leans over one arm and raises other arm off floor. This is like driving on one wheel. Return to stable position and lower to mat. Switch places.

VARIATIONS:

Can you balance on the other hand?
Can you raise the free hand high overhead?

4. Flat Tire

DESCRIPTION:

Partners take wheelbarrow position. Wheelbarrow is told that tires hit a nail. Slowly bend elbows and lower chest to floor. Psssss, the air goes out. Now tire must be pumped up. Wheelbarrow pushes shoulders upward until arms are straight again. Switch places.

VARIATIONS:

Can you stop the flat halfway down and pump it back up?
Can you pump up the tire if hands are wider than shoulders?
Can you pump up the tire if hands are close enough that thumbs touch?

5. Dump the Dirt

DESCRIPTION:

Partners take wheelbarrow position. Wheelbarrow fills up by raising hips higher than head, then dumps the dirt by raising one foot out of partner's hand and bringing it up overhead. Carefully bring foot back to partner. Lower to mat. Switch places.

VARIATIONS:

How high can you raise the free leg?
Can you straighten the free leg?
Can you change to use other leg?

Series

After children learn several different movement patterns, they enjoy putting the patterns into a series of two or three consecutive movements.

1. Can you do a *seat kicker*, then a *forward roll?* Can you do a *forward roll*, then a *seat kicker?*

2. Can you do a *barrel roll*, then a *forward roll?* Can you do a *barrel roll*, then a *back shoulder roll?*

3. What other movements can you put together in a series?

Opposing Files

Children enjoy opposing files because they find it exciting to pass each other while executing a skill.

Children stand in a file facing forward toward and to the right of another file of children facing them. The teacher first

announces which movement pattern will be executed. Then the first child in each file responds to "Readyyy . . . Go!" For example:

1. This time, when your turn comes, everyone do a *forward roll*. First two, readyyy . . . Go!

2. This time everyone do a *seat kicker*, then a *forward roll*. Readyyy . . . Go!

Quick Follow

Children love the excitement of fast movement. The important prerequisite is that the movements must be very familiar to the children before they can do them quickly and avoid collisions. In Quick Follow, the children stand in a file. The first one executes a movement, then quickly gets out of the way so that the next child can do the same movement at the same spot on the mat. In this way the children follow one after another in quick succession.

1. When you hear the command, "Go," the first person will do a *forward roll* and go to the other end of the mat as quickly as possible. As soon as the person in front of you is out of the way, you execute the *forward roll* without a command as quickly as you can. Readyyy . . . Go!

2. This time, when you hear the command, "Go," the first person will do a *barrel roll* as quickly as possible. Everyone follow in turn. Readyyy . . . Go!

3. Use other movements that the children like, making sure that the children are very familiar with any movement to be used in Quick Follow.

Shuffle the Deck

Few things are more exciting than a near miss. Children who have become familiar with Quick Follow will enjoy Shuffle the Deck.

Two files of children face the same mat at 90° angles to each other. The first child of one line executes (for example) the *front roll*; the first child in the other line follows closely behind (but not so close that they kick each other or collide) and executes the same or another movement. In this way members of the two files alternate, or Shuffle the Deck. At first this should be done slowly. After the children are familiar with the movements, they can, and usually do, go much faster. The teacher must constantly supervise this activity.

6. Supplement for the Teacher or Parent in Training

Children and Physical Skill

Because of extensive changes in our life-styles, there is reason to be particularly attentive to the physical development of our children. Any generation faced with major cultural adjustments will need energy, vitality, and physical skill to succeed. Yet, without a conscious effort on our part, the next generation could actually have less personal energy with which to live their lives.

A Change in the Way Children Play

Recent events in our culture have changed the way our children play. Advancements in labor-saving technology and changes in family life-styles have greatly reduced a child's opportunity to develop physical skills. Television and video games are designed to capture children's interest and have served to reduce immensely the number of hours spent in gross motor activity.

In years past, children were able to develop physical skills through play in the natural environments of our communities. Children spent long hours playing in the streets, vacant lots, and fields near the home. Play was the dominion of children, a tradition experienced and carried out by the youngest members of our society. Jumping rope, spinning tops, chasing folded paper airplanes, playing marbles, and playing jacks were but a few of the many activities that filled the child's world.

Older brothers and sisters and children in higher grades seemed always ready to act as instructor, coach, and referee. Younger children learned from these older children how to make kites and stilts, to cut out rubber guns, and to play stick ball and buck buck. As they grew older, these children would in turn pass on the skills to those in the grades below them. Through this system a "culture of childhood" was passed from one generation to the next and it was through this system that many children developed enough physical skill to get them through the rest of their lives. But this is true no longer.

Young children of today do not receive their motivation from older children but are under the influence of the day care employee, television, and other children their own age (because they are grouped by age in the day care facilities and in the schools).

When children play with older children a few grades ahead, there develops a hierarchy of command, so that the more mature take responsibility to teach or guide the younger. The younger children look up to the older children as heroes and as role models. But when all children are near the same age, the most skilled and aggressive ones are not teachers but competitors. And when one child demonstrates skills that the others cannot match, the effect is for the less skilled to retreat to a safer environment where they will not be put down. This situation leaves a great many children lacking in skills that they could easily learn, skills that would provide each child with a greater range of choices in work and leisure time. Thus, the "culture of childhood" has been disrupted, our children have lost their natural teachers, and the quality of physical skills in our nation is in jeopardy.

Learning through Movement

Physical movement and physical skills play a major role in the life of young children. In the very beginning of life, movement provides children with a sense of self. Movement fills the body with sensations. Movement gives rise to a sense of being alive. Swinging the arms and kicking the legs are the child's primary means of getting a taste of what it is like to be a human being.

For the newborn it is a real adventure to thrust the arms and legs into space in search of what might be there. And the rush of sensations generated by this action sends back the signal: It is me; I am what is here and I am alive.

It does not take long for the thrusting motions to become planned actions. Knocking over a toy may at first be happenstance, but the pleasure of seeing the consequence of movement soon results in premeditated action. Movement becomes the tool by which children can investigate their world. What will fall over and what will stand firm? What can I pick up and what just feels gushy? What is soft and what pricks the hand? A million things are there to investigate and each has its rewards and consequences. And movement is the medium through which all of this adventure and learning can take place.

Growth and maturity quickly bring children into the stage of being mobile. Movement can literally bring children into new and different worlds. The quality and precision of movement become of primary importance. By not falling down steps one can get farther, see more, and avoid pain and disorder. And if one can move the arm and hand just right, the knob on the door will turn, the door will open, and—Whoooa—a completely new world of things to see, feel, and investigate.

The child not only uses movement for mobility, but now must also learn to read the meaning of the movements of others. The frown on a parent's face, the raised hand, the upturned lips of a growling dog all become signs of impending events to be avoided. The smile on a grandmother's face, the kissing and touch of a mother or father are signs that the world is in order. Thus, movement becomes a medium of expression and communication. The child learns to read the expressions of others and then finally begins to use movement as a means to express his or her own feelings.

Moving into new worlds brings on an unexpected and somewhat abrupt value for movement skill. Here and there are things—dogs, other children, pot plants balanced on pedestals—things from which one needs protection. Certain things can fall, strike out, or actually attack when one is investigating a new world.

The quality and skill of movement are now translated into the ability to protect oneself. Children's physical skill literally protects them from the hostile elements in the environment. With agile movements they can dodge a swinging fist, climb out of reach of an aggressive child, or possibly avoid a barking dog or an irritated adult.

Likewise, movement skill provides the basis for adventure, allowing children to move into the uncharted areas of life that give meaning to what is best about being human, the ability to discover and to learn through one's own efforts and curiosity. Natural curiosity gives everyone a desire for adventure, but only those with a sense of self-confidence can follow that curiosity out into the environment. The child who follows a butterfly to the edge of a creek can continue the adventure only if his or her physical skill is sufficient to leap over the water, accurately land on a rock, and then maintain balance and control. Physical skill and the experience and confidence to use it become the basis for an adventurous life. And these experiences into uncharted territory are what give depth, width, breadth, and fullness to being human. It is the uncharted experience that makes one life different from another. These experiences are what give an individual a sense of uniqueness and self-worth.

Thus, we see that for a young child physical movement is the source of discovery, the vehicle for expression, and the method of survival. The skill with which physical movements are carried out becomes a measure of the quality and fullness of a child's life.

Skills for a Lifetime

Few adults can balance on a log or swing on a rope or execute a cartwheel better as an adult than they could as a child. Most of these basic body control skills are learned during childhood play. And for most people these childhood skills are all we will have to take us through life. We often refine some skills, such as driving a car or typing or playing a musical instrument, but the basic ability to control our body, maintain balance, and exhibit agility and coordination has previously been learned during the physical play of childhood.

Childhood offers each individual a unique opportunity to develop physical skills. Children run, jump, roll, and climb for the sheer pleasure of the kinesthetic sensations. In very young children, there is little concern for how they might look to someone else. This lack of concern for how one looks to others enables a child to experiment with all kinds of body positions and movements and physical challenge. However, the social freedom to enjoy this spontaneous experimentation does not last long. Very soon the social pressure to look "cool" and in control prevents people from taking a chance on falling down or experimenting with unique physical activity. When an individual loses the social freedom to enjoy spontaneous movement, this signals the end for improving basic physical abilities. The narrow range of physical activity within which individuals must live their lives has been set.

Americans have traditionally developed their repertoire of physical abilities during childhood play. But childhood in America has drastically changed in recent decades. Should it happen that coming generations lose a substantial portion of their physical ability, it could reduce our nation's capacity to participate in new and adventurous projects and it could reduce our energy and vitality as a people. And if we are to adjust to the immense cultural changes going on in our society, we will need an abundance of energy and vitality.

Brain Research and Education

It has long been suspected that physical play had some direct relationship to cognitive abilities. One could understand that the ability to visually track a ball was somehow related to the ability to visually trace a line of words across a page of print. We could see that certain physical components to cognitive skills might be enhanced by practicing physical activities. But somehow this does not fully explain the relationship. Something more is involved and not until recently have we been able to find the clue.

New research on brain function suggests that our ability to think and be creative is highly dependent upon stimulation of the right half of the brain, which gets a substantial portion of its input from the kinesthetic sensations of physical play. Research is showing that the brain has at least two systems for processing information. One system, which is usually related to the left side of the brain, processes information in linear, step-by-step fashion. This system handles mathematical and verbal information that can be categorized and named and labeled.

The brain has a second system for dealing with the more complete perceptions that pour in as a barrage of sensation. This process is usually associated with the right side of the brain and deals with a panorama of sight and sound and the kinesthetic sensations of the body in motion. This is the system necessary to link such phrases as "jump a rope" or "fall off the diving board" with the feelings that accompany these experiences. This is the part of the brain that gives a third and fourth dimension to our cognitive and emotional life.

This perceptual side of the brain is also linked with our capacity for creative thinking. It is said that our most creative thinkers have a very full development in and a special appreciation for at least one of the great sources of perceptual input: music, art, or physical activity.

Albert Einstein is known to all for his mathematical abilities. Only a few are aware that his ability in music was so developed that he was considered a virtuoso violinist. Many of his experiments were carried out only in his mind, visualizing falling elevators and speeding trains and what might go on inside them. When his perceptual ability was coordinated with his mathematical ability it brought about ideas that have changed our world.

When most of the world sees something in the same way, it requires a certain uniqueness to see it differently. When one has the facility to literally see or feel the world upside down it brings on new and sometimes very useful viewpoints. The perceptual ability to see things inverted or reversed is demonstrated by the invention of the assembly line. In Henry Ford's time, one would build something by establishing a location and then bringing materials to that site. But this system did not work well when Ford wanted to build many automobiles exactly alike. Consequently, Ford had to see things reversed. Instead of having the builders carry materials to the site, he conceived of having the site brought to the builder. This ability to reverse the traditional procedure created the assembly line, an invention that changed American industry.

In order to maintain a reservoir of unique creative ability in our population it is necessary to ensure a full development of the kinesthetic sensations and perceptual capacities of the brain. This development does not occur in our graduate schools, but rather in our kindergartens and child care facilities.

A New Responsibility

There is little chance of bringing back the "culture of childhood." Child care facilities are apt to remain the primary institution for raising preschool children. For good or for ill the opportunity for our children to develop kinesthetic perceptions is now under almost total control of the adult supervisor.

This major change in the nature of child rearing demands that specialists in physical development take on a new responsibility. No longer can we rely on the playground and free time for the physical development of future generations. Children must have a guided opportunity for physical development just as surely as they depend on a guided program of immunization or a guided program to learn numbers and language. If children are to reach their potential, there must be a conscious and ordered curriculum directed by professionals dedicated to that purpose. This is the new responsibility of those who would participate in the raising of our children. This is the new responsibility of those who see children as our nation's most important natural resource.

A Fresh Look at Our Objectives

People are imbued with an adventurous spirit and a curiosity that drives them into uncharted and unpredictable experiences. People are forever wanting to walk on the moon, to climb down the face of a cliff, to photograph an eagle in its nest, to ski down a mountain, to swim across a channel, to look for unusual rocks in rough terrain, and to follow their interests and curiosity wherever they may lead. To move about and manipulate our environment is our way of understanding ourselves. Physical education is simply acquiring the physical skills necessary to follow one's curious and adventurous spirit. No one wants less from life.

Our objective then as physical educators is to provide each

human body with an opportunity to develop its natural physical ability. This is accomplished by stimulation and development of the kinesensory systems that coordinate incoming sensory information with outgoing muscle responses. These include the systems for balance and for orientation in space, as well as the motor areas of the brain that program the sequence of muscle contractions necessary to produce coordinated patterns of movement.

We should avoid competitive situations that serve only to identify the elite athletes. We should find ways to give every child ample opportunity to enjoy spontaneous physical play. We should put physical challenges into their proper instructional sequence so as to facilitate learning. And, finally, we should find ways for children to experience teamwork so as to learn the value of cooperation.

To properly fit into an educational system the plan should be based on an orderly progression of skills. Progression provides direction for the program because it identifies the initial steps, the content of the program, and the future goals that we wish to achieve. A plan based on a progression of skills could also provide at least a basic continuity of program between one community and another, which is important in a mobile society like ours.

Progression in a program also increases participation because children can experience the feelings of pleasure and success at each step before going on to the next. These feelings of success encourage all children to participate and continue in the program. Progression ensures that each child will more nearly reach his or her full potential.

Gymnastics: A Place to Start

Basic gymnastic activities provide the best medium with which to start our program. Developmental Gymnastics provides a variety of physical challenges that encourage the development of agility, balance, and coordination. Gymnastics is based upon control of the body, as well as the timing, position, balance, and coordination of its movements. In Developmental Gymnastics, children learn to turn their bodies over both forward and backward, to balance while inverted, and to develop agility both upright and inverted. As children participate in these activities, the motor and sensory systems in the body are provided an excellent opportunity to develop basic functional relationships. The sensory systems begin to coordinate with each other, and the children become more aware of their body as an extension of their mind. Further, many basic movement sequences are developed and stored that can be used in sports and other situations in later life. It seems natural, then, that we should use Developmental Gymnastics activities as a way to begin developing physical skills for children.

Theoretical Basis of Physical Skill

Physical skill does not just happen; it is an orderly process that develops step by step by step. All those interested in child development need at least a basic understanding of how patterns of movement are organized and controlled by the child's neurological system. A better understanding of the organization and control of movement is necessary to properly analyze movement patterns and to plan programs for their development. Such an understanding will improve our ability to guide children in the development of physical skill.

The Units and Organization of Movement Patterns

The great neurophysiologist Sir Charles Sherrington once referred to the motor nerves in the spine as the "Spinal Keyboard." From this we can take our cue as to the makeup of physically skilled movements.

The movements of the body parts are organized similar to the way in which music is written. In music, for example, the basic element is the note. Notes are put together to form chords, and chords are written in sequence to develop the musical score. The movements of children can be described in a similar way. The positions of individual limb segments are the "notes" of movement. The total body configuration, or posture, is the "chord" of movement. And the sequence of postures that the body goes through to execute a movement pattern is the "melody," or "dance," of the movement.

This analogy can also be described in terms of the muscle activity that is required. The muscle action that brings a particular joint to its proper position is defined as a *motor note* and is the basic element of body control. The combination of actions that brings all joints to proper position for a particular posture is called a *motor chord.* The sum total of all muscle actions that move the body through a planned series of postures is called a *motor pattern.*

Thus we see that skilled movements are not a haphazard contraction of muscles but, rather, an organized and predictable set of events:

Motor notes   bring individual body parts to their proper position in a posture

Motor chords   coordinate the many simultaneous muscle actions to ensure the proper form of a posture

Motor patterns   carry out a sequence of postures that flow together to form a skilled movement

Observing after the Fact

For those working daily with children whose very nature is to run, scamper, kick, wiggle, throw, and dodge, this comparison of movement to notes and chords may seem far too simple. Children move so quickly and so fluently that one seldom sees the individual body postures. Movement rather than posture is the most observable characteristic of children because we are observing the children after they have already learned the body positions and have become masters at quickly and easily moving from one to the other.

However, the requirements necessary for children to skillfully execute these movements are indeed similar to the requirements for skillfully playing a measure of music. One cannot play a measure of music without being able to play the chords that go together to make it. One cannot play the chords without being able to reach each of the notes that make up the chords. And, although a musical score is made up of individual notes and chords, it can sometimes be played with such skill that the qualities of rhythm and flow transcend the qualities of the individual notes.

The movements of children are executed in a similar fashion. Children cannot skillfully perform a movement pattern unless their bodies can execute the postural positions that make up that movement pattern. The postural positions cannot be executed unless the individual joints can assume their proper positions in the posture. But if the children have learned the motor notes that bring each joint to its proper place and if they have developed the motor chords that coordinate the many joint movements into the proper posture, they will be able to execute movements that flow from posture to posture with no visible transition.

The Development of Motor Notes

Children of elementary school age are literally bursting with movement patterns that flow out with the slightest provocation. However, anyone who has been responsible for a baby during the time when the baby was learning to eat with a spoon, put an arm through a sleeve, or tie a shoelace can attest to the fact that control of movement develops ever so slowly. In fact, control over the body parts is gained one motor note at a time.

The newborn baby must learn to control its body by giving conscious attention to each body part individually. Through conscious attention to what is observed, a baby can control a limb to a certain destination—the thumb to the mouth or the hand to a pacifier. If the movement that is performed results in a desirable reward, it will be repeated again and again as long as the reward remains desirable.

After a number of awkward attempts the movement will become smooth and more accurate. Through continued repetitions the baby learns to bring the thumb exactly to its target—not overshooting or undershooting, but right on target. After a few more repetitions it will be observed that the baby no longer monitors the details of the movement. A *conditioned response* has been developed. The force that is exerted, the distance that is covered, and the speed with which it is carried out have become preplanned. The thumb can be brought to the mouth even though the baby is obviously concentrating on and visually observing other events. Responsibility for directing the muscle action has been transferred from conscious control to subconscious control, which is able to repeat the movement with extremely good consistency.

These often-repeated movements whose control becomes subconscious and whose characteristics are prearranged and extremely consistent take on the quality of a motor note.

The Development of Motor Chords

Even for the very young baby, the action of a single limb movement will not be sufficient to meet its needs for long. It soon becomes desirable to sit up and to play with a toy at the same time. The simultaneous control of several sets of muscles is the next step in the baby's skill development.

The important characteristic of the control system here is that, once the details of the force, distance, and speed of a movement have been worked out, the responsibility for control can be transferred from the conscious to the subconscious level. The process by which control of the characteristics of a muscle action is transferred from the conscious to the subconscious level can be called *motor programming.* It is this process that makes possible the simultaneous control of two or more muscle actions.

Take, for example, the problem that a baby of six months faces in trying to sit erect and play with a toy. To accomplish this requires one set of muscle actions to keep the trunk upright in a sitting position and another set of muscle actions to direct the hands to the toy. However, the conscious mind of the baby can concentrate on only one concept at a time. If the baby concentrates on getting its hands on the toy, its body will fall over. If the baby concentrates on keeping balance in the sitting position, it is not free to play with the toy.

Since both sitting erect and playing with a toy have their own individual rewards, the baby will work at them one at a time. The baby will sit upright again and again for the pleasure of seeing and hearing more. And, while lying on its back, the baby will shake a rattle for the pleasure of sight, sound, and feel. Through this repetition the muscle actions required to hold the trunk in the sitting position will become programmed and will no longer require the baby's attention. Now the baby can sit erect with the conscious mind free to concentrate on playing with a toy.

Thus, we see that motor programming provides the means for the establishment of motor chords. Once a motor note has been established it can become part of a motor chord when its association with other motor notes produces a desirable result. This simultaneous control represents a great improvement in the baby's body-control capacity. At three months the baby could "play" only by extending an arm toward an object (using motor notes), but by the eighth month the baby can play by sitting erect and holding an object (using motor chords). Thus, we see several sets of muscles being controlled simultaneously. This is the beginning of body posture. These are the first motor chords being formed.

By observing skilled movements carefully, one can learn to identify the postures that are critical to their success. These postures then become objectives in themselves. Most of the skills described in Developmental Gymnastics are actually postures that are necessary for some more-complex skill further up the progression of difficulty. In some cases two, three, or four steps are required to develop a particular motor chord. One also recognizes that the development of certain motor chords must wait until children reach an appropriate level of physiological and perceptual maturity.

The Development of Motor Patterns

The movement patterns of skipping, throwing, kicking, and swinging, which we see daily on the school playground, are actually planned sequential arrangements of motor notes and chords that the children have previously learned. At this point it does not seem apparent that these notes and chords were painstakingly learned one at a time. However, these patterns were not always so smooth and easy.

The protective environment of very young children provides them the opportunity to move from one posture to another with great deliberation. The one-year-old toddler learning to walk may prepare for a number of seconds before leaving the security of a chair to step and reach for mother. Moving from one balanced posture to another requires careful consideration and planning. Here again we find that, if a specific sequence of postures consistently produces special rewards, this sequence will be practiced again and again. Here, too, we find that, if the requirements of postural sequence and timing are consistent, the motor programming process can transfer control from the conscious to the subconscious level.

Thus, we see that the sixteen-month-old child not only has learned to walk but also can do so while visually tracking and reaching for a balloon. From this point on, the child can move about the environment adjusting postures one note at a time or adjusting motor patterns by changing the sequence or by adding new chords.

By the time children have reached the first grade it seems as though they have a virtually endless repertory of new and different movement patterns. And, to be sure, most have learned to chase after a ball, dodge the angry hand of parents and teachers, and throw erasers at both friends and enemies. But a more careful analysis will show that a large number of children never learn to climb a rope, pull their body up over a bar, or jump down safely from waist height in spite of the fact that such patterns of movement are well within their capacity and would add greatly to their choices of work and leisure throughout life.

It is appropriate now to apply this understanding of organizational control to the analysis of movement patterns in order to plan programs to facilitate skill development.

Analysis of a Movement Pattern

Careful analysis of a movement pattern will show that there are certain reference points in the sequence of events. At these reference points all parts of the body are brought into a very specific configuration, or body posture. Thus, we can describe a skilled movement by the postures that mark the sequence of events. The forward roll, for example, can be described by five identifiable postures, or reference positions:

1. The knees bend into a squatting position
2. The hands reach the floor and take some of the weight in an all-fours position
3. The body becomes inverted as the head is ducked and the hips are lifted over the shoulders

4. The rounded shoulders and neck then roll up over the feet to a squatting position
5. The legs are extended as the body comes to a standing position

Each of these postures is an important part of this particular movement pattern. And, even though it is possible to change or bypass one of these postures, this is the sequence that most children will follow in performing this particular pattern.

Each of these postures can be described by the position of the individual limbs and joints. For example, in the posture listed as no. 4, the knees are bent and the body is bent at the hips, so that the heels nearly touch the seat and the knees nearly touch the chest, and the arms are reaching forward. The position of each individual body part goes to make up this body posture, which is critical to the success of this particular movement pattern.

A Pictorial Sequence Is Not an Educational Sequence

Too often we try to teach by having children attempt to follow the pictorial sequence of a gymnastics skill. Take, for example, the cartwheel. In the illustration we see that the performer begins with arms raised overhead and steps forward through a straddle handstand and on over to a standing position. In the absence of an educational sequence, an instructor will often attempt to have children imitate this pictorial sequence by having them practice standing with arms raised overhead. Then the children are encouraged to reach down with the arms while kicking forcefully up and over in an attempt to imitate the second and third position in the pictorial sequence. This is not proper as an educational sequence. Following this procedure will show that a few children (maybe 15%, who are natural athletes) do in fact learn the cartwheel. But most children

(about 80%) will try, fail, and go away feeling that they just are not skilled enough to be a gymnast.

An educational sequence, however, would give every child in the class a way to develop the necessary body postures and balance positions to accomplish the cartwheel. Young children should be learning (a) how to raise the leg above the head (steps 1, 4, and 7 of the Inverted Agility sequence), (b) how to bring the leading leg back quickly to the floor for support (steps 2, 5, and 8 of Inverted Agility), and (c) how to hold the center of gravity behind the plane of the arms (steps 3, 6, and 9 of Inverted Agility). By following this procedure and allowing children time to develop a conditioned response, about 98 percent will in fact accomplish the cartwheel.

Thus, we see that an educational sequence is designed to prepare children by giving them the opportunity to develop the necessary body postures (motor chords) prior to attempting the skill. This is similar to teaching addition of numbers as a prerequisite to multiplication. This is the system necessary if we are using gymnastics as a base for lifelong skills as opposed to using gymnastics solely as a means of identifying those who would be good gymnastic athletes.

Kinesthetic Preview

When the limbs of the body are placed in a desired posture the performer receives a rush of kinesthetic sensations related to that position. The trace of that sensory nerve activity will remain for a few seconds. Therefore, it is often very useful to have students take the desired finishing posture just prior (within a few seconds) to the action that will initiate the movement. In this way the performer can more easily recognize the proper position if and when it is attained.

Developmental Gymnastics: How It Works

Preschool children do not have the necessary motor chords to execute the forward roll in its entirety. When a pattern of movement requires a motor note or chord that a child has not previously developed, the missing elements must be learned separately and established in the subconscious control system before the desired patterns can be attained. Therefore, we begin development of this physical skill by teaching children activities that stimulate development of the various motor chords that are required.

In Developmental Gymnastics the progression leading to the forward roll consists of five steps. The children begin with the first step and then play with each step in turn until it is mastered before going on to the next. (These steps are fully described and illustrated in the Novice and Intermediate portions of this book.)

Step 1. The first step in the forward roll development is the *scamper*. Here children learn to support their weight on the arms. This activity develops strength in the arms and allows children to become familiar with having weight on the arms with hips above the head. It is important that children practice the many variations.

Step 2. The second step in the forward roll is called the *back rocker*. The children learn to rock up and down the back and to feel the shift of weight from shoulders to hips. This posture must be a very well established motor chord in order to achieve success with step 5.

Step 3. The third step in the forward roll is called *look behind*. The children look back between their legs with hands and toes on the floor. This posture is a challenge to the orientation system in the inner ear. When the children feel comfortable with this posture, they are able to use the kinesthetic information from their hands and arms, which are not in their visual field. When this posture is mastered, the basic motor chord for posture 3 in the forward roll is established.

The teacher should be aware that just getting the body into a certain posture is not the same as establishing a motor chord.

A posture is not a motor chord until it can be held by subconscious control, leaving the conscious attention free to direct variations of the activity. It is important, then, to allow children plenty of opportunity to play with each step and to experiment with all the variations.

Step 4. The fourth step in the forward roll is called the *tip over.* The children look behind with the head placed on the mat and raise their hips until they fall over the head. The *tip over* helps children learn to anticipate the sensation of the back and hips hitting the mat on the other side.

Step 5. The fifth step in the forward roll is called the *seat lifter.* The children learn to bring their chest up close to their knees and to keep their feet back under their knees. The weight shifts from the buttocks to the feet. For primary-age children this is a very difficult motor chord and should not be strongly emphasized. Their heads are heavy, their legs are light, and it is difficult for them to establish the rotational momentum that is required. The second- or third-grade child who has learned steps 1, 2, 3, and 4 during a previous year will have no problem accomplishing this movement.

Chords Make the Pattern

Mastering these five steps completes the preparation. With this background of motor chords a child will accomplish the forward roll in its entirety on the first or second try.

In the program of Developmental Gymnastics the activities listed are in every case important motor chords. One chord builds upon another in a progressive sequence to form more intricate physical skills.

It should be noted, however, that in the presentation of these movements each step is named and given an identity of its own. None of the movements should be considered as less important than another. To progress from step 2 to step 3 should be considered just as important as progressing from step 8 to step 9.

Movement Amplification

Movement amplification is another way to use motor notes and chords to expand and enhance physical skills. Whereas a progression list predetermines how the notes and chords will eventually be put together, movement amplification introduces whatever additional note or chord seems appropriate to the situation. Thus, if a child can jump over an obstacle with ease, the teacher may ask, "Can you jump over while holding a ball in your hands?" Or, if a child can execute a forward roll with feet side by side, the teacher may ask, "Can you come up with one foot in front of the other?" With only two or three changes a very simple and common pattern can become an unusual and skilled movement. Further, the changes can be made in a direction that favors the skills of that particular child. Providing children the opportunity to amplify their skills can produce interesting and sometimes exciting results.

An Environment for Learning

To develop an enjoyable learning environment that will stimulate a class of children is truly the teacher's greatest task. To take a group of children to a room, gymnasium, or playground does not ensure that each one will "tune in" to the teacher's plan for physical activity.

The behavior of children is motivated by numerous factors and, although the desire to play and to explore the world of physical movement is a major factor in the motivation, it is certainly not the only one. Failure of a child to participate in the activities as planned could be the result of any number of factors, for example:

Perceptual and motor control factors	failure to receive or understand instructions and cues
	lack of the motor chords that are required to produce a reasonable chance of success
Physiological factors	lack of strength
	lack of endurance
Psychological factors	being disturbed by a bad experience in the previous class or earlier in the day
	fear that a poor performance will cause teasing from peers
	fear of the activity because it has previously been associated with danger
	trying to get attention by not succeeding or cooperating
	lack of ability to translate what is seen and heard into physical movements

Observation Is a Form of Participation

Often a very young child will simply sit and observe the activities of the class. This is a child who needs some time to assimilate what is being seen and heard. This is not an uncooperative child. This child can usually be seen executing the activities seen in class at some other time during the day, maybe at home with parents in the evening. It is important not to rush this child into activity. It is appropriate to ask the child, "Would you like to try?" But do not insist because the child is taking in as much new information as possible for the moment. Some children will sit for a month or more before they become so familiar with the environment that they can join in with the others in side-by-side play. But this is a very important month. Children should not be rushed or pushed past this period of observation.

With these many and varied motivating factors operating, it is no easy matter for a teacher to get the entire class interested and involved in the plan of the hour.

The Power of Success

Much can be done to develop a good atmosphere for learning physical skills by taking advantage of the great motivational power of success. Be assured that an undeserved compliment is not success. An undeserved "A" is not success. Success is having a specific objective and reaching it. Success is knowing that you reached it. Success is having your friend or teacher tell you that you reached it after you already know inside that you did.

Successful experiences can turn a child from a "you have nothing that I care about" attitude to a "please let me do that again" attitude. The rewarding feelings that accompany the successful accomplishment of a new physical skill often overpower the various nagging problems that can beset the many children that make up a class.

An atmosphere of success will also benefit the teacher. Because of the cooperative attitude that results, less time is required for class management and the teacher can spend more time helping individual children and providing enrichment for the class. A series of successful experiences can develop a class momentum that brings teacher and children together with a feeling of mutual respect. Teaching becomes less pressure and more pleasure.

To ensure that children will find success requires a series of just-right physical challenges, each of which builds upon the other.

A Progression of Skills

As we plan a unit of physical activities, successful experiences should be a built-in factor. The class should begin with an interesting activity that the children can already do and then quickly move into new challenges that are still within their capacity to accomplish.

To conduct such a lesson the teacher needs a list of skills, each of which builds upon the other by adding just one new motor note or chord. If the new task requires only one new motor element, the child can consciously guide the body parts with the visual or kinesthetic senses. The other parts of the task are already controlled subconsciously, and with a few tries the additional requirement will fall into place. However, if the new task requires two, three, or more changes in the child's existing motor patterns, it will be difficult to coordinate all the new movements. Success will be much harder to find, and in many cases the child loses interest and quits trying. It is often difficult to obtain a progression list on any one particular physical skill, but a good list is essential in planning a unit on physical skill development.

Challenge without Threat

The "just right" task that will inspire an enthusiastic response from the class is a valuable tool for the teacher. For the children such a task is an exciting experience that raises the senses out of boredom but does not cause anxiety or fear. This middle ground between boredom and fear is that essential ingredient of learning called challenge. A challenge is a task for which there seems to be a solution. Students are stimulated by a challenge. They want to try because they are reasonably sure they can succeed. Inside they feel that "this is something I can do if I'll just try."

Without the guide of a progression list physical skills can quickly lose the qualities of challenge and instead become either boring or a threat. When a child is missing three or four of the motor elements required, a task can become threatening. A threat is a task or obstacle for which the child sees no solution. Children and adults alike learn to avoid such situations whenever possible. The inner feeling is, "If I try this I'll just look dumb; I'll fail it for sure."

On the other hand, none of us want to try something that does not have any interest for us. We want to tackle something that has at least some challenge. We want to take a little risk in order to reach out further into the uncharted areas of life. This element of risk and the unknown is a great motivating factor and is an important element in challenge.

When the steps in a progressive sequence come too fast for the children, they feel threatened. If the steps come too slowly, they become bored. The key to good teaching is to provide a just-right challenge for every student. This demands a step-by-step progression that spans the spectrum of abilities within the class.

Variations in Ability

In every class the teacher finds that the children will vary considerably in their ability to perform. This is not the exception, but rather the general case. In fact, if skill enlarged the portion of the body associated with it, the average class might look like the one pictured here.

Some children have developed more in their physical capacities than in their verbal ones, others more in language than in mathematics; some are sociable while others are very antisocial.

The teacher should not expect all children to perform activities in the same manner or at the same level of skill. It is important to allow children plenty of freedom to change and vary from the task as presented. The many variations that normally occur should be accepted and recognized as having their own unique contribution.

Skill progressions such as those listed in this book will help the teacher to provide every child with a challenge to fit his or her particular skill level. The first step in any progression should be one that all the children can accomplish. This ensures that each child has something he or she can perform. Succeeding steps should be progressively more challenging and should be taken fast enough to prevent boredom. Enough steps should be taken so that most students are aware of the line of progression and are challenged by some part of it. The more advanced students, like all the others, should have freedom for their own variations and expressions of skill.

The Growing Edge

Depending on age and previous experience, children will have arrived at various levels of skill on any progression list. *That point along a progression list at which a child has presently arrived defines the child's growing edge. This is the point at which learning can best take place.* This is the point that identifies those tasks that will be too easy, those that will be too hard, and those that will be just right to encourage maximum growth and learning.

Every class will have some children at the higher and some

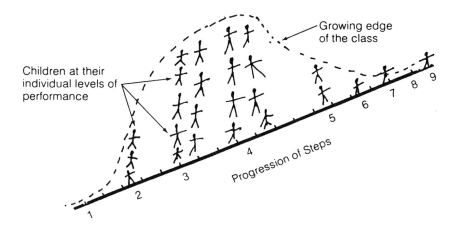

children at the lower levels of performance, with the rest falling somewhere in between. It is important for the teacher to find that point on the progression list which represents the growing edge of the class as a whole. This is the point around which the class can find some common feelings. It indicates the steps that will be the just-right task for the greatest number of children. It is the point where the momentum of success can best be achieved. This means that most children will be occupied with constructive activity, thus providing the teacher more freedom to spend with individuals at either end of the spectrum.

A parent or teacher should not compare one child's ability with another's. Each child will have his or her own growing edge and rate and priority in learning. It is very natural for children to vary in this way. It is impossible to predict where any particular child will be on the progression ladder at any particular age. Those who have no opportunity to practice may not move up this ladder at all even though their bodies continue to grow and mature in size, weight, and strength. Skill depends upon experience. The teacher's comments about a child's behavior should be made in comparison only to that child's previous behavior.

Freedom from Ridicule

Since the growing edge of each child is unique for that individual, growth and performance will be also. If all children are judged by the same criteria some children will receive rather harsh judgment. When children are critically judged against a standard of performance they cannot attain, the result is ridicule.

Many children fail to learn physical skills simply because their initial awkward attempts are met with ridicule. Children who receive this response either will quit trying or will continue to work under undue pressure to succeed. For a class to develop a healthy atmosphere conducive to learning, ridicule

and belittling statements must somehow be controlled. The physical education class is not the place to emphasize what a child does wrong. Rather, it provides an excellent opportunity for a child to play without being judged. Here children who may seldom meet with success during other parts of the school day can receive praise for their successes.

The Inverted U-Curve of Performance

We can all note that there is in general a positive relationship between a child's attention to the task and the child's ability to perform that task. However, there is a point at which too much attention can actually reduce performance. When increased concern about a task reduces performance, it is called the inverted U-curve as shown here.

When a child wants to succeed in order to gain adult approval the child will want to do better and may concentrate on the task. But when the adult withholds approval to the extent that the child feels great pressure to succeed, this pressure can actually become distracting and reduce performance.

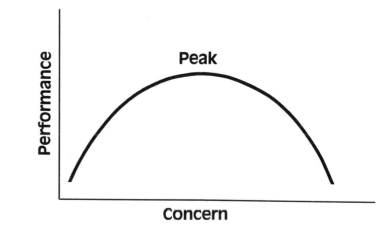

When a child realizes that failure on a task will bring an angry response from an adult, the child will attempt to do better. But concern about the adult's anger causes inhibitor muscles to become increasingly active and eventually the performance level begins to drop. When a child realizes that failure could cause a bad injury, the child will attempt to do better. But again fear causes the inhibitor muscles to become increasingly active and eventually the performance level drops. Researchers in performance psychology have noted that too much concern over the results of performance actually causes performance to drop. In sports events the player who cannot perform near his or her potential is said to "choke." The great teachers and the great coaches are those who can get their students to focus on the task at hand without becoming overly concerned about the consequences.

The Value of Acceptance

The thrill of being upside down or holding a tripod balance for the very first time can only be exceeded by the feeling of having that feat of skill recognized by teachers and friends. This recognition confirms the child's feelings of self-esteem.

For some adults it may be difficult to give acceptance to one child for a tripod when most other children in the class are doing headstands. To honestly accept any specific performance one must constantly be aware that growth can take place only at a child's growing edge. It is the process of growth, development, and learning that one should recognize. This makes it possible to accept any improvement in performance as having value regardless of where on the progression list the child may have started.

Genuine acceptance can do more to nurture growth than possibly any other human communication. Accepting each child for his or her unique worth is the greatest gift the teacher can give.

Motivation from Within

The greatest motivation is that which we feel from within. Whenever possible children should be allowed to interject their own imagery into the play. The image of leaping over a river or riding on a floating log is a powerful motivation that calls forth all of the previously learned movement patterns. In this self-motivated situation the child responds with all of his or her abilities, not just that which is necessary to satisfy a nagging adult. This complete focus of attention produces a rapid learning rate and a full, rich experience.

Breaking the Code of Childhood

Learning to communicate with children requires that we break the code of childhood, which to adults is truly a foreign language. One important difference between childhood communication and adult communication is the reference words that key our responsive mode. We adults respond to the names of those in high political office or famous writers, actors, or scientists and those whom we feel have power or influence over our lives. Children respond to a different group of reference words simply because there is a different group that holds influence over the world in their mind. Famous cartoon characters, heroes of children's story books, and mommy and daddy are the persons of their world. Words of action that directly describe their personal activity and the images in their mind are also key to breaking the code of childhood. Once an adult learns to speak in the language of children, learning and love grow rapidly and the time spent together becomes a pleasure.

Be Sure to Have Fun

Physical activity is naturally fun and interesting for children. Whenever possible the teacher should allow the spontaneous feelings of happiness and fun to remain a part of the class atmosphere. Since we as adults have passed through the stages of childhood long ago, it is sometimes difficult for us to identify with these spontaneous feelings. Children are full of stories and imagination and make-believe, while we are required to make payments on an automobile, pay rent, and deal with our own relationships in the world. Yet, an environment for maximum learning will be fun for both the children and the teacher. When children enjoy the class, there is likely to be more physical activity during the class period and the children are more likely to resume the activities on the playground and in their neighborhoods.

When the teacher and the children enjoy the class, development of physical skill can be more fully integrated with development of personality and other aspects of life. The process of developing physical skills can truly become a bright spot in the educational environment.

Presenting a Lesson in Developmental Gymnastics

The program of Developmental Gymnastics consists of a number of movement patterns on tumbling mats and other apparatus, each of which is presented as a series of progressive steps. The steps are listed in the order that best facilitates learning. Generally, but not always, each step is a little more difficult than the previous one. For example, the steps in the Inverted Balance sequence are as follows:

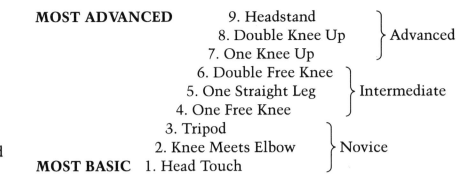

The tumbling mat program consists of seven such lists, each list covering its own particular type of movement pattern.

The children are presented these activities one step at a time. As the children become familiar with the movement at a particular step and can perform the movement and its variations, they will want to progress to the more difficult steps. However, each step in a progression is named and should be presented and enjoyed for its own qualities. No one step, regardless of its number, should be considered as more important or valuable than another.

When a child does not have success with a particular movement, he or she should play with the preceding movement and all its variations. When the right combination of experience and maturity has been reached, a new step up the progression list can be accomplished in only a few tries.

A class with no previous experience will find that the novice-level activities are a good beginning challenge regardless of grade level. Most kindergarten and first-grade children will complete the novice but probably not the intermediate program. Most second- and third-grade children will complete the intermediate but probably not the advanced program. Nearly every fourth- through sixth-grade child who has had the novice and intermediate programs during previous years will be able to complete the advanced program.

Planning Lessons for Grades K, 1, and 2

Children in kindergarten and the first and second grades should be presented only one step in a sequence on any one day. These primary-age children need plenty of time to work on all the variations at each level. They should be given time to invent, explore, and receive recognition for their own unique variations. The first day's lesson, then, might consist of three activities. The *scamper* (step 1 from the Turning Over Forward sequence) could require five or ten minutes of class time; the *knee slapper* (step 1 from the Upright Agility sequence) will take less time because it demands a more intense expense of energy; and the *head touch* (step 1 from the Inverted Balance sequence) will require five to ten minutes of class time. These could be thought of as three mini lessons, a mini lesson being all the activity related to a particular progression sequence.

Children should be allowed to play with a mini lesson as long as it is interesting and stimulating to them. But before a movement loses its appeal, the teacher should move on to another mini lesson. Changing to another mini lesson before the children become bored will maintain their interest and they will be eager to come back to the activity later.

During the second lesson it is good procedure to review the previous step and take up one new step in each of two or three progression lists being presented. By using this procedure the entire novice program on tumbling mats can be covered in five lessons. If the children are having a high rate of success, continue into the intermediate program.

Planning Lessons for Grades 3, 4, 5, and 6

Children in the third, fourth, and fifth grades can usually recognize the relationship between one step and the next in a progression. For them, the first day's lesson might consist of two mini lessons, each one involving all three steps in the novice program. These children will find the novice program relatively easy and will want to move quickly through it. When they are into the intermediate and advanced programs, however, it will be helpful to spend a day on each of the steps.

A lesson should consist of two, three, or possibly four mini lessons, depending on the length of the period. Again, the teacher should change the activity to a new mini lesson before the children lose interest. It is good procedure to review the previous one or two steps as a part of each mini lesson. By using this procedure the novice and intermediate programs can be covered in seven to ten lessons. If the children are having a high rate of success, continue into the advanced program.

Presenting a Lesson

Physical skills can be learned only by actual practice. Therefore, each child needs a place of his or her own in which to practice the movements. The children should spread out around or in front of the teacher on mats or on the grass outside.

WARM UP:
   A moment or two of warming up can make the children receptive to movement challenges, establish the teacher as the source of the challenges, and prepare the nerve and muscle systems for movement. No more than one or two minutes will be needed for this. Any movement that is easy for every child is appropriate. Such movements as bouncing up and down on both feet, straddling the feet, and bouncing on one foot at a time serve this purpose very well. The teacher should change the movement several times so that the children develop the habit of responding to the teacher's directions.

ISSUE A CHALLENGE:
   Present the first step of the first mini lesson either by demonstration, by having a child demonstrate, or by showing the appropriate illustration. The challenge should be in terms

of the children's interest and vocabulary. This is an important technique that makes the class more fun by appealing to the imagination of the children and teacher alike. Children in the first two or three grades respond well to a challenge to mimic animals. For example, a good challenge might be, "Who can hop like a bunny?" Older children are more responsive to references to current television heroes, such as Wonder Woman, or to football heroes from the nearest well-known team.

ALLOW TIME FOR RESPONSE:

The children will want to respond to the challenge. Give them time to try, encouraging them to try several times. If the movement is easy, issue variations of the challenge, such as "Can you hop over a creek?" "Over a log?" "Around your mat?" and so on.

ACKNOWLEDGE INDIVIDUAL CHILDREN:

While the children are trying the movement, call attention to them individually. Acknowledge both the so-called correct responses and the variations, for example, "You got your leg up very high, Johnny," "That was good balance, Carol," and "Look, Bill found another way to do it."

ISSUE THE NEXT CHALLENGE:

After the children have enjoyed the movement and its variations for a few minutes, give them a signal, ask them to stop, and have them sit on their mats so they will be able to hear and understand the next challenge. By this procedure, one can usually cover about three mini lessons in a twenty-minute period.

FREE TIME:

Near the end of the class the children need time to experiment and show off their skills. Have them sit down and ask if any of them would like to show the class some movement they know. Allow two or three demonstrations, one at a time. Then invite all the children to spend a few moments practicing any movement they wish.

DISCUSS THE LESSON:

A short discussion will do much to integrate physical and cognitive development. Children can be asked to name the new movements they have learned. They can be asked to tell what a movement feels like to them. Then suggest that they can learn to spell and write the names of the movements and, perhaps, use them in a sentence or story. Also suggest that they show their parents what they have learned and tell them what the skills are called.

Stations

When working with larger groups of children it becomes necessary to establish teaching stations in order to properly use the various pieces of gymnastic apparatus. If more than six children must take turns on a piece of apparatus the waiting time provides opportunity for various distractions. Therefore, a large group of children can be divided into a number of smaller groups and each small group can work at a station. In this way five stations can accommodate thirty children.

Since young children do not easily remember complicated instruction, it is important to make the assignment at each station very easy to remember. A picture or a description of the assignment on the wall next to the station will often help them to stay on task.

Children should not stay at any one station for more than a few minutes. The changing of stations tends to bring children back on task and realign them with the objective.

Floor Work

As the teacher makes the assignments for each station the children should be given a feel for what the skill will be like. Children can "pretend" that they are on the apparatus and make every movement that is possible to accomplish in their space on the floor. This floor work is in effect kinesthetic instruction. It is very important in helping children to anticipate what the movement will be like. Further, it greatly improves the child's chances of success, especially when working on a skill that has not been attempted before.

Floor work also helps keep the students' attention directed toward the instructor. When a physical response is required it prevents distractions and keeps the children focused on the subject at hand. The alert teacher will use floor work to prepare children for every apparatus.

Class Organization, Supervision, and Safety

In order to develop a program that will be accepted by parents, administrators, and the community, the program must be well organized and safe for the children. The following guidelines will be helpful in planning such a gymnastics program.

Curriculum

The curriculum used should be presented to the children in a developmental order. This order of developmental sequence is one of the primary emphases of the Developmental Gymnastics program. Be sure to present the activities in order and allow the children time to become thoroughly familiar with each movement before moving on to the more difficult activities.

Individual Space—Fall Zones

One source of problems occurs when one child falls into another. This can cause injury and it almost always diverts

class attention and focus away from the intended activity. One very good way to prevent children from falling into each other is to provide each child with an individual mat. Spread the mats apart sufficiently to create a "fall zone" so that when children do fall they will not collide with each other.

Distribute the mats according to how much space is available and how many children must be accommodated. For small classes a semicircle is an excellent way to arrange the mats. For larger classes concentric semicircles or lines may be more appropriate.

If individual mats are not available strip mats can be marked to separate fall zones and children can alternate using the space.

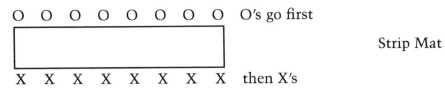

O O O O O O O O   O's go first

Strip Mat

X X X X X X X X   then X's

Space around Apparatus

When apparatus is used, there should be sufficient space to ensure that children from another station will not wander into the fall zone. Some configurations that are known to work well are illustrated here.

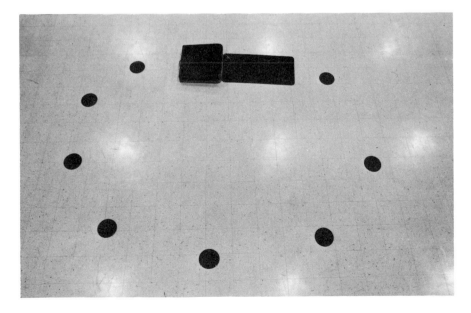

When working with very young children it is useful to mark the flow of movement with "safety spots" or some type of marking on the floor. This procedure tends to help keep children within the flow of movement around the apparatus.

Any protrusions, obstructions, or columns in the activity area should be properly padded and called to the attention of the children.

Supervision of the Activity

When children are physically active around apparatus they must be constantly supervised. The best supervisory techniques are those that keep the children focused on their task and thus reduce the opportunity for distractions.

Playing background music can help reduce the effective noise level during the use of stations. The interruption of the music can be used to signal a change in stations or it can be a signal that some instruction is coming from the teacher. The playing of background music and using music interruptions as a signal for instructions is one very effective technique for getting every child's attention in a short amount of time.

The teacher cannot assume that activity and learning will continue in an orderly manner should he or she leave the room. Therefore, the teacher must always remain in the room during physical activity and must lock the door or put the equipment away when the class is over.

Another very important technique of supervision is for the teacher to visualize the class in action. This visual rehearsal can help one to anticipate disruptions and thus take steps to prevent the disruptions from happening. The more visual rehearsal the teacher does the better will be the flow of the class and the less likely there are to be injuries and problems. For example, a teacher might visualize putting on the music and remember that during the last class the cassette needed to be rewound, then remember that it was while the cassette was being rewound that several of the more rowdy children got into a scuffle. This visual review might remind the teacher to have the cassette rewound prior to the start of class. Or it might remind the teacher to have a pencil in a particular location, or to have pictures taped to the wall by the stations, or any number of other things that make the class flow better and allow more learning to take place. In any case, the teacher who practices visual rehearsal will be more prepared to supervise the class activity.

Safety Factors

The American Association of Educational Gymnastics Teachers published the following list of safety factors. Any teacher of gymnastic activity should carefully consider each point.

1. NONCOMPETITIVE ENVIRONMENT:

Children should be taught in an atmosphere of learning and self-motivation rather than comparing their performance to that of other children. Although children often do compete with each other, this natural tendency toward competition should never be used by the teacher as a prime factor in motivation.

2. ACTIVITIES TAUGHT IN LISTED ORDER:

The skills should be listed in the order in which they are to be learned for maximum safety and success.

3. CONDITIONED RESPONSE:

Children should begin with the first level of difficulty. Before a child is allowed to move to a higher level of difficulty he or she should first develop the present skill to the point of a conditioned response, that is, the movement can be successfully performed by subconscious control. This is determined by having the child use the conscious mind to conduct a simple task, such as counting "1, 2, 3, etc." or spelling "J-o-h-n," during the performance of the physical skill and watching for deterioration of the performance.

4. PROVIDE SUFFICIENT SPACE:

The most probable cause of injury is one child falling into or against another child. To prevent this teachers should give each child sufficient space within which to move without interfering with other children.

5. PRIOR KNOWLEDGE OF DISABILITIES:

When children enroll in a program the teacher should obtain a medical release stating any disabilities that the child might have and any precautions that must be taken by the teacher to ensure the safety of the child.

6. AN ATTITUDE OF RESPECT:

We believe that the most effective deterrent against injuries is an attitude of respect for the children on the part of the teacher. Further, the teacher should require the children to respect each other and the instructional environment.

If a teacher carefully attends to all of these safety points, the children will have a very delightful and safe place in which to learn gymnastic activities.

The American Association of Educational Gymnastics Teachers

In 1985 the Texas State Board of Education required for the first time that every elementary school child must receive instruction in Sequential Gymnastics and Tumbling. This requirement brought a new and challenging responsibility to the teachers of young children in Texas. The American Association of Educational Gymnastics Teachers (AAEGT) has now formed to assist in the implementation of that law and to encourage other states to adopt a similar one. For information call 512-458-8427 or write Box 4548, Austin TX 78765.

A Focal Point for Educational Gymnastics

The purpose of the AAEGT is to provide a focal point for the promotion of educational gymnastics for the young child. While there are many associations dedicated to children and at least a few dedicated to gymnastics, no organization has as its primary focal point the kinesensory development of young children. The AAEGT holds that the development and integration of the sensory and muscle response systems is so important for the growing child that it deserves the primary attention of a national organization.

A Shortage of Teachers

The AAEGT recognizes that there is a great shortage of teachers who are qualified to work with children in the area of motor development. Adult employees often do not consider themselves as candidates to teach motor development, and five years of college training costs too much for the pay schedule of the teacher on the line in the child care facility. Yet there are those who enjoy the physical play of children and would be excellent supervisors and guides with the proper in-service training.

Teacher Certification Course

The AAEGT has developed a certification system so that employees of day care facilities and teachers of preschool and elementary school children can be trained quickly and efficiently. The AAEGT sponsors teacher certification in Developmental Gymnastics as a model program of the educational type. The certification course is divided into preschool, primary, and elementary levels. Each course requires sixteen hours and is usually conducted over a weekend. For information call 1-800-955-1439.

Program Continuity

A further reason for encouraging the Developmental Gymnastics curriculum is to provide continuity for children who move from one community to another. Day care facilities in many cities in Texas offer this curriculum and, therefore, children who move from one community to another can often continue the program right where they left off. This continuity should be available in every state.

To Identify and Encourage Kinesensory Development

Many programs already exist that work toward the development and integration of the sensory and muscle response systems in children. An important objective of the AAEGT is to identify those programs that use a sequential approach and to assist in their promotion throughout the nation. To assist others in the development of curriculum, the AAEGT has published the following list of curriculum criteria.

1. *Safety* must be inherent in the sequential nature of the program and included in the teacher training system
2. *Sequential* lesson plans should be listed in the order in which the skills are to be taught
3. Movement skills should be grouped according to common *neuromuscular patterns*
4. *Variations* for each activity should be listed to encourage the internalization of the skills
5. *Internalization of skills* is very important before children proceed to the more complex movement patterns
6. *Spacing between steps* should be of appropriate size to accommodate every student going through the program
7. The categories of movement chosen should emphasize *fundamental abilities* of the human body

8. A *noncompetitive* environment should be developed in order to emphasize self-reliance and self-confidence
9. Programs should be *co-educational* at the preschool, primary, and elementary levels to simplify equipment and teaching requirements

For Information Concerning Teacher Certification or Membership

The AAEGT welcomes inquiries and/or new members. Those interested should write to:

American Association of Educational Gymnastics Teachers
Box 49065
Austin, TX 78765
Or call 512/244-1439

Obtaining Equipment

The equipment used in developmental programs, such as Developmental Gymnastics, should be very simple so as to emphasize the activity of the child rather than the complexity of the apparatus. When children are to climb on equipment it must be stable and resist falling over. The equipment can often be improvised by the alert teacher, with safety being the primary concern.

To obtain a brochure on the equipment used in the Developmental Gymnastics program, write:

Physical Fun Products, Inc.
Box 4548
Austin, TX 78765
Or call 512/836-5238

Bibliography

Bilodeau, E. A., and I. M. Bilodeau. *Principles of Skills Acquisition.* New York: Academic Press, 1969.

Eckstein, Gustav. *The Body Has a Head.* New York: Harper & Row, Publishers, 1970.

Edwards, Betty. *Drawing on the Right Side of the Brain.* Los Angeles: J. P. Tarcher, Publisher, 1979.

Fits, P. M., and M. I. Posner. *Human Performance.* Belmont, Calif.: Brooks/Cole Publishing Co., 1967.

Lawther, J. D. *The Learning of Physical Skills.* Englewood Cliffs, N.J.: Prentice-Hall, 1968.

Montessori, Maria. *The Formation of Man.* Thiruvanmiyur, Madras: Kalakshetra Publications, 1983.

Rasch, P. J., and R. K. Burke. *Kinesiology and Applied Anatomy.* 4th ed. Philadelphia: Lea & Febiger, 1971.

Ruch, T. C., H. D. Patton, N. W. Woodbury, and A. L. Towe. *Neurophysiology.* 2d ed. Philadelphia: W. B. Saunders Co., 1965.

Sherrington, C. *The Integrative Action of the Nervous System.* New Haven: Yale University Press, 1906.

Suzuki, Shinichi. *Nurtured by Love.* Athens, Ohio: Senzay Publications, 1969.

Thompson, Richard. *Foundations of Physiological Psychology.* New York: Harper & Row, Publishers, 1967.

Williams, Linda. *Teaching for the Two-Sided Mind.* New York: Simon & Schuster, 1983.

Outline of Activity Program

Program of Mat Activities

Novice	Intermediate	Advanced
UPRIGHT BALANCE		
1. The Friendly Crab	4. V-Seat	7. Knee Lifter
2. Knee Balance	5. Front Support Balance	8. Bent Hip Scale
3. The Mechanical Toy	6. One-Foot Balance	9. Extended Hip Scale
FALLING AND LANDING		
1. Back Rocker	4. Dog Roll	7. Standing Sit Back
2. Seat Roll	5. Sit Back from Squat	8. Back Shoulder Roll
3. Puppy Dog Roll	6. Sit Back to Dog Roll	9. Paratrooper's Fall
INVERTED AGILITY		
1. Leg Lifter	4. Kick Up	7. High Kick
2. Leg Switch	5. Switch-a-Roo	8. Switch-a-Roo-Roo
3. Straddle Switch	6. Barrel Roll	9. Cartwheel
INVERTED BALANCE		
1. Head Touch	4. One Free Knee	7. One Knee Up
2. Knee Meets Elbow	5. One Straight Leg	8. Double Knee Up
3. Tripod	6. Double Free Knee	9. Headstand
UPRIGHT AGILITY		
1. Knee Slapper	4. Seat Kicker	7. Straddle Knee Touch
2. Ankle Slapper	5. Straddle Jump	8. Straddle Toe Touch
3. Twist and Leap	6. Stride Leap	9. Pike Jump
ROLLING OVER FORWARD		
1. Scamper	4. Tip Over	7. Forward Roll from Scale
2. Back Rocker	5. Seat Lifter	8. Step—Leap—Forward Roll
3. Look Behind	6. Forward Roll	9. Reach Over—Forward Roll
ROLLING OVER BACKWARD		
1. Back Rocker	4. Arm Roll	7. Shoulder Balance
2. Back Balance	5. Back Rocker to Arm Roll	8. Backward Straddle Roll
3. Back Rocker to Puppy Dog	6. Back Shoulder Roll	9. Backward Roll

Program of Springboard Activities

Novice

FORWARD BOUNCING
1. Jump Off
2. Knee Slapper
3. Seat Kicker

TWISTING
1. Bouncing Up
2. Bounce and Turn
3. Around and Back

ROLLING SEQUENCE
1. Land, Then Squat
2. Land, Then Bunny Hop
3. Land—Bunny Hop—Tip Over

WITH TABLE
1. Land On—Jump Off
2. Land On—Knee Slapper Off
3. Land On—Seat Kicker Off

Intermediate

4. Tuck Bounce
5. Straddle Bounce
6. Stretch Bounce

4. ¼ Twist
5. ½ Twist
6. ¾ Twist

4. Knee Slapper—Tip Over
5. Seat Kicker—Tip Over
6. Seat Kicker—Forward Roll

4. Rebound
5. Rebound—Knee Slapper
6. Rebound—Seat Kicker

Advanced

7. Straddle Leg Touch
8. Pike Bounce
9. Pike Leg Touch

7. Rebound
8. Reverse Stand—½ Twist Off
9. ½ Twist On—½ Twist Off

7. Pike Bounce—Forward Roll
8. Straddle Bounce—Forward Roll
9. ½ On—½ Off—Forward Roll

7. Bounce to Tuck
8. Forward Roll over Tumbling Table
9. Roll On—Roll After

Program of Low Horizontal Bar Activities

Novice

SWINGING UNDER
1. Hang and Swing
2. Hang and Walk
3. Back Up to Standing

SUPPORT ABOVE BAR
1. Front Support
2. Space Walk
3. Knee Bender

GRIP CHANGES AND TURNING
1. Over Grip Hand Walk
2. Mixed Grip Hand Walk
3. Turning in a Circle

Intermediate

4. Run Under
5. Run Under and Arch
6. Squat—Kick over Line

4. Knee Touch
5. Toe Touch
6. One Leg Over

4. Mixed Grip Space Walk
5. Reverse Grip Space Walk
6. Front Support Slide

Advanced

7. Squat—Kick over Rope
8. Underswing over Line
9. Underswing over Rope

7. One-Leg Balance
8. Sitting Toe Touch
9. Alternate Legs Over

7. Single Leg Over—Hip Swivel
8. Single Leg Cuts
9. Single Leg Over—½ Turn

216

AROUND THE BAR

1. Front Support
2. Hip Hug
3. Bar Hang

4. Flexed Arm Hang
5. Hanging Ball
6. Front Roll

7. Leg Curl
8. Assisted Back Pull Over
9. Back Pull Over

ROTATING UNDER THE BAR

1. Toe Touch
2. Knee To Chest
3. Bat Hang

4. Toe Hook
5. Skin the Cat
6. The Basket

7. Single Leg Swing Back
8. Double Leg Swing Back
9. Single Leg Uprise

HIP CASTING

1. Front Support
2. Double Leg Swing
3. Cast Away

4. Seat Kicker
5. ¼ Turn Dismount
6. ½ Turn Dismount

7. Cast to Tuck
8. Cast to Pike
9. Cast to Straddle

Program of Tumbling Table Activities

Novice

Intermediate

Advanced

VAULTING OVER

1. Crawl
2. Scamper
3. Side Bunny Hop

4. Switch-a-Roo
5. Straddle Switch
6. Barrel Roll

7. Bounce to Tuck
8. Bounce On, Then Over
9. Bounce Over

ROLLING FORWARD

1. Log Roll
2. Puppy Dog Roll
3. Tip Over

4. Kick Roll Up
5. Roll Up—Straddle
6. Step, Jump, Roll Up

7. Forward Roll—Level
8. Straddle Roll—Level
9. Pike Roll—Level

ROLLING BACKWARD

1. Seat Balance
2. Back Rocker
3. Toe Touch

4. Hands on Mat
5. Tip Over Backward
6. Backward Roll

7. Straddle Back Roll
8. Backward Roll
9. Back Roll, Then . . .

Program of Beam Activities

Novice

BALANCING ON THE LEVEL BEAM
1. Step On and Over
2. Balance On
3. Step to the Side

VAULTING ON THE LEVEL BEAM
1. Front Support
2. Sidewinder
3. Dancing Crab

BALANCING ON THE SLANTED BEAM
1. Walk to First Mark
2. Slide to First Mark
3. Go Backward to First Mark

VAULTING ON THE SLANTED BEAM
1. Bear Dance
2. Bear Bounce
3. Turning Toy

Intermediate

4. Walk Forward
5. Slide to the Side
6. Walk and Pivot

4. Crab Vault
5. Step Over Vault
6. Barrel Roll

4. Walk to Second Mark
5. Slide to Second Mark
6. Walk Backward to Second Mark

4. Step On Vault
5. Tuck Bounce
6. Kangaroo Hop

Advanced

7. Cross Over
8. Jump Switch
9. Twist-Jump

7. Step Through
8. High Barrel Roll
9. High Kangaroo Hop

7. Ball Carry
8. Ball Toss
9. Turn While Walking

7. Knee Balance
8. Squat Balance
9. Squat Mount